In 1944, before very many ttle in
the Western Arctic, Jim and Be   h old
son, Jamie, took up residence at Fort Liard, south west of Yellowknife
in the Northwest Territories. Jim had cheerfully volunteered for a
return commitment with the Royal Canadian Mounted Police and
Betty, a physical education teacher, looked forward to the new experience with an adventurous spirit, tempered by trepidation. Jim's job
was to uphold the law and to provide clearance for the export of furs.
He was also appointed Indian Agent. The only other non-native families were those of the Hudson's Bay Company Factor, an independent fur trader and later, a Game Warden.

Forget running water; forget electric lights; forget schools,
churches and supermarkets. Conditions were primitive to say the least,
yet the Reids stayed for six years, the author departing the community only for the birth of two sons, David and Patrick.

"You learned to take nothing for granted, to take no chances
with your health and safety. You had to be vigilant against the conditions, the weather, to survive," Reid says. "But I loved the peace and
quiet, the simple lifestyle and the absence of controversy."

Most of all, the writer fell in love with the native people—fur
trappers and their families from the Slavey Band whose cultural beliefs and moral values built in them a "great integrity and dignity of
spirit."

Elliot Lake resident Betty Reid is a born story teller. Her collection of first-hand sketches of family life in the Far North of the
1940s, is sprinkled with both humour and pathos, and well worth the
read.

Linda Wilkins

This project is a true story based on the lives of a 'Canadian
Mountie', his wife and family. It is written by a wife, mother and
partner, as well as a friend of others.

The story begins prior to World War II when Jim and Betty
Reid made the decision to accept a posting to the Northwest Territories. It describes the pleasures and hardships of life in that time and

1

in that part of Canada. It is written from the heart and viewpoint of a full partner to her husband's activities and responsibilities as a government authority. It describes how, with consideration for others, two very diverse peoples can work and live in harmony when mutual respect exists. These stories demonstrate how co-operation could exist between Canada's First nation people and authority when respect and consideration for each other exist. The stories describe the conditions and some of the hardships encountered. Less is made of the hardships with more emphasis placed on people relationships and "good times."

It is a story of people and how they coped and reacted to an experience which few citizens of this great land will ever experience. The characters in these stories are all real and lived during the events of the book.

Peter Cousins

Betty:

This is only my opinion, but I think your project is important. It is the best picture I have seen of how a Mountie functioned in the Northern settlements. He was doctor, confessor, law-keeper, and most of all, a comforting presence to all who lived in the community. Needless to say, his wife played an important role in everything.

It is immensely important to preserve such stories for posterity. The least we can do is to make sure a complete manuscript is in various archives and certainly in the RCMP Archives.

So please keep going with it. It is indeed worthwhile.

So long for now,

Sam Holloway, Editor, Yukoner Magazine

Bitten By The 'Arctic Bug'
Reflections of an RCMP Officer's Northern Life

by Betty Reid

White Mountain Publications

©2003 by Margaret Elizabeth Reid (Betty Reid)

Box 5180
New Liskeard, ON
P0J 1P0

www.wmpub.ca

Cover Photo ©Tony Sharp courtesy of
North Nahanni Naturalist Lodge,
Box 807 Fort Simpson, NT X0E 0N0
For other spectacular photos and information go to:
www.nnnlodge.com

National Library of Canada Cataloguing in Publication

Reid, Betty, 1921-

    Bitten by the 'Arctic bug' : reflections of an RCMP officer's
    northern life / Betty Reid.

Includes index.

ISBN 1-896331-55-6

    1. Reid, James. 2. Reid, Betty, 1921- 3. Fort Liard (N.W.T.)—
Biography. 4. Royal Canadian Mounted Police—Northwest Territories—Fort Liard—Biography. I.Title.

FC4199.F63R44 2003   971.9'3   C2003-903051-2
F1060.92.R44R44 2003

Canada Council Counseil des Arts
for the Arts   du Canada

We acknowledge the support of
the Canada Council for the Arts
for the production of this book.

ISBN: 1-896331-55-6

Printed in Canada

Dedication

James N. Reid

1913 - 1999

I dedicate this collection of stories to the memory of my late, wonderful husband, James N. Reid.

He was a devoted husband and father and a most honest person both in action and intention. He was not only a gentleman but also a gentle man in all his expressions and actions.

Our married life of fifty-eight years was never marred by petty differences or indifferences. He is sorely missed by his family.

But with children, people never really die!

Jim Reid with Governor-General Massey and Mr. Robertson, Commissioner of the North West Territories Presentation of the Mace in Ottawa on Parliament Hill

Acknowledgements

This collection of stories never would have materialized without the guidance and support of gifted friends, especially Barbara and Peter Cousins. Barb, with her infinite patience, surpassed only by her computer skills and foresight that was so much relied upon.

My appreciation to Allan Gibbons who spent many hours correcting my mistakes with such skill and tact. His recommendations were of the utmost importance to me.

I am also indebted to my wonderful daughter, Cindy, whose encouragement and support were most helpful.

Last, but certainly not least, my thanks to Basil Jesshope who introduced me to creative writing and provided me the encouragement to pursue it.

Thank you to everyone, I really appreciated your help.

Betty Reid

Table of Contents

Why Go North

"Do you really think you'd like to go North? It's for three years you know, not just a weekend." My husband of two years, looked at me closely, waiting for my answer.

Jim and I became engaged while I was attending the University in Toronto. He had joined the Royal Canadian Mounted Police (RCMP) several years before, had served in the North and also had been part of the Musical Ride in Ottawa for two years. In those days a Mountie had to be in the Force for seven years before he could marry. Even then, he had to obtain permission from the commissioner of the RCMP. And let me tell you, my retired Army Major/ father did not exactly appreciate having his daughter's background investigated before permission to marry was granted. But it was the order of the day and that was that. With three years remaining Jim decided to go north, serving at Arctic Red River and Aklavik to put the time in. While he was there, I taught Physical Education at Acadia University in Nova Scotia for the winter and worked for the Navy in Halifax during the summer.

And now his three years were up. He was coming home or 'Outside' as he called it, meaning civilization as we know it.

Three years engaged to someone and never seeing them in all that time. Would we feel the same? What if he had changed? What if he thought I had? Excited? Naturally, but apprehensive too. I received word that he would arrive in Halifax the next afternoon. What a long morning! Finally, the doorbell rang and I rushed down and opened the door.

There he stood, seeming to be taller than I remembered. His blonde hair was streaked by the sun and his arms tanned brown. Actually that's what really hit me—how hairy his arms were! But he was the same person I had fallen in love with three years before.

It took a few days to become comfortably acquainted again in order to make decisions. We decided on an October wedding as Jim

9

had to report for duty then in Regina. We were married down east in Westville, Nova Scotia and left immediately for Depot Division, Regina, Saskatchewan, where we were posted for two years. During that time, Jim taught swimming and life saving to Navy and Air Force personnel and I taught at the YWCA.

It was while we were in Saskatchewan that our son Jamie was born—born to a couple of 'experts' who took nearly an hour to get his first diaper folded properly, but after this stuttering start, we managed to progress quite favorably.

During this time I could tell Jim was still enthralled with his life in the Far North. He spoke of it often and kept in touch with friends both on the eastern Arctic as well as the western Arctic, so when he asked me if I'd like him to apply for Northern Service, I readily agreed. After all, we would get fifty cents a day extra pay and it would be a new adventure for me. I enjoyed the outdoors and was an avid hunter and canoeist. I thought it would be a great challenge.

Eventually, we were posted to an isolated place called Fort Liard in the Northwest Territories. It was about eighteen hundred miles from Edmonton in the area of Nahanni that was famous for its Deadman's Valley, sometimes called Headless Valley. The Police had decided to reopen the neglected Detachment because some of the younger men belonging to the Slave Band of that area had become a bit aggressive. They had had twelve years with no police intervention and the two non native families living in Fort Liard grew more and more alarmed at their errant behavior. One family involved was a man called Jack Sime, an Independent fur trader, along with his wife Peggy. The second was the Hudson's Bay Company Manager, John Forrest and his wife Bea. Both families had infant daughters. These two families had businesses to run and came in contact with the natives daily. There were non-natives along the river who had settled there several years ago and they were also becoming uneasy at the defiance shown by some of the young men and were requesting protection from Ottawa.

"Why would a person 'volunteer' to go North? One would have to be an absolute idiot to offer to serve in the Far North. If you are being punished and that is your sentence, well, that is a different kettle of fish. But that life's not for me." Such was the statement I overheard while attending a conference on Northern Affairs. I guess it was a popular conception because several friends and a few tactless relatives asked us why we had consented to go to an RCMP Detachment that had been closed for more than twelve years—a place so isolated that it received supplies once a year by freighter with mail flown in four times a year: March, July, October, and of course, December. That didn't seem too intimidating at the time but in future we would feel isolated in between deliveries as there was no direct communication to the outside world except when the Hudson's Bay Company manager made contact on a daily basis by wireless each evening at six o'clock. We would be two hundred miles from the nearest doctor and hospital, either at Fort Nelson in British Columbia or Fort Simpson on the MacKenzie River. Travel would be by canoe or if possible, by plane in the summer and dog team in the winter.

Indeed, why? Well you see, when my husband had been posted up North at Aklavik and Arctic Red River previously, he had been bitten by the 'Arctic Bug.' It festered into a chronic longing to return to the North. So we did. In fact, we stayed for a total of six years.

We had many preparations for our move. Food supplies for the first year were provided by the Police quartermaster stores. The head of ordering must have been a young unmarried member. We received cases of certain articles such as skim milk and salty stew and then only a dozen essentials but we survived. Our three month old son's supplies consisted of six hundred pounds of baby food, several dozen cans of spinach and liver which never did sit well anywhere. As rations were not supplied for children, we had to purchase these ourselves.

I asked Jim where we could purchase additional supplies if they were needed. He replied that we'd likely be able to get a few articles at the Bay store in Fort Liard but we had to bear in mind that food supplies would be received only once a year, when the Northern Transportation supply boat made its annual trip.

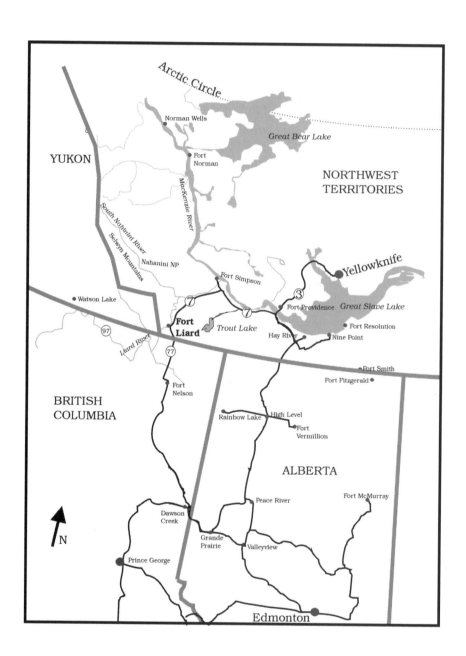

The Journey Begins

Our trip began in Regina, Saskatchewan, on May 24, 1944. We boarded a train and traveled to Edmonton, Alberta. From there, we took the second slowest train in Canada. The track was built on muskeg and the train rippled along at a crawl. Some passengers said they actually got off the front car and picked berries until the last car caught up and then they hopped back on.

While in Edmonton, nine other RCMP members joined us at the station. They too were going to different Northern postings at Chipewyan, Providence, Vermillion, Simpson and Norman Wells. Only one other member, Vern Teeple, was married.

Mounties enroute to their new postings

Arriving at Fort McMurray, we weren't inspired by the surroundings. Shacks had mushroomed to accommodate workers at the Tar Sands project. When you looked around, you could see doghouses with dejected looking sleigh-dogs tied alongside. There were also two hotels, one which we were directed to, and a couple of restaurants. So with bag and baggage we straggled into our temporary lodging.

Downstairs in this hotel we entered a large room equipped with a huge, long bar and behind it were dozens of bottles of every drink imaginable—all alcoholic. Along the front base of this highly polished bar was a brass rail on which you could rest a foot while enjoying your drink. Every five feet or so were shiny brass spittoons, and the floor around it bore the evidence that it wasn't always a dead hit. We had never seen such a bar so naturally we all visited this oasis. The regulations in Alberta were that the bar could serve customers from ten o'clock in the morning until four o'clock in the afternoon; then it was closed until 6:00 p.m. During that off period, the glasses were washed and the place tidied up. All the tables were covered with glasses of beer as it was sold by the glass, ten cents each with the traffic to the bar being constant.

We spent two days at Fort McMurray before making a portage by bus to Fort Smith. There we were scheduled to catch the boat north downstream on the MacKenzie River. What a disappointment to learn that we had missed the supply boat by only one day! The boat had left two days earlier to deliver freight to Aklavik and it wouldn't be back for at least ten days. We were getting a little discouraged as we were looking forward to the last leg of our trip.

Two weeks dragged by and the boat finally returned. It had been pushing a barge with tons of freight and got stuck on two different sand bars. Still, we enjoyed our stay at Fort Smith. The other members were put up in the hotel but we were more fortunate. Because we had a three-month old baby we were invited to stay at the Detachment living quarters. The Sergeant's wife was out visiting in Edmonton.

While there, I seized the opportunity to bake a cake. Having been married in wartime, it was difficult to get supplies; things such as butter, sugar and chocolate were strictly rationed, not to be wasted on a beginner. So I decided to make a cake when no one would be looking over my shoulder. All seemed to go well until I mistook a bottle of oil of citronella for vanilla. That ruined it but since I wasn't aware of my mistake, I went ahead and baked the cake. When it came out of the pan, it was hard as a rock.

Now visiting the Detachment that afternoon was Inspector Birch, en route down-river on an inspection trip. Poor unfortunate man, he had just been a dental patient having had most of his teeth extracted. Unsuspecting, he helped himself to a piece of my cake and I couldn't help but notice that more than once he dunked his cake in his tea. Still, the gallant old English gentleman thanked me profusely and sucked down his treat.

While at Fort Smith the RCMP members were approached by the Game Warden to assist him in an investigation regarding contraband beaver. Pelts were being shipped out illegally and the source couldn't be traced. Armed with a search warrant, the men made a search which led them to an oil company. There they came upon rows of oil drums presumably full of oil. The men each took a row and checked for any empty ones. Jim tipped one sideways and it was lighter than the others. They continued their search and found two dozen drums to be filled with beaver pelts, all stuffed up in through the bottom. The manager of the oil company, not satisfied with supplying the North with oil, had resorted to an illegal traffic of smuggling furs, costing him his license and his livelihood.

While waiting to resume our trip, we were treated to a story which was related to us by the Sergeant in charge.

It seems the Commissioner of the Royal Canadian Mounted Police was on an inspection trip. While in Fort Smith, the Sergeant naturally was expected to entertain his Commanding Officer so he invited him to dinner one night. Unfortunately, the Sergeant was called out while his wife was finalizing preparations. She had set the table in the dining room putting out the salt, pepper and pickles, all the time trying to keep her four-year-old son out of the Commissioner's way. The kindly gentleman said the child was no bother and he answered the many questions asked by the lad as the little boy followed him into the dining room. Across the table the Commissioner spotted the tray of dill pickles and helped himself to one.

"Oh sir, sir" shouted the little boy. "Don't eat that, sir! It'll shrivel your dink."

The boy's mother overheard the warning and froze in her tracks. Mortified, she had the presence of mind to slip over to the outside door, quietly open it and then slam it shut. Humming a tune as loud as she could, she pretended she had just come in. Later told her husband she was sure her heart had actually stopped. She was assured by her husband that probably the Commissioner had heard a lot worse in barracks, and really, the boy was only looking out for the gentleman's welfare.

"That's okay for you to say," retorted the wife, "You weren't there!"

Betty Reid aboard the freighter.

Finally, with our belongings and freight on board the freighter, we began the last leg of our journey. At certain points along the MacKenzie River, we would pull in to shore and drop off an RCMP member at his new home, some looking a little woe-be-gone but they would adjust in short order.

On Great Slave Lake, it seemed we got stuck on every shifting sand bar, but with the heavy diesel motor, we were able to back off and free ourselves. One night Jim and I were up in the wheelhouse with Captain Barney Goodman, and I wondered out loud if it was too early to go to bed since it wasn't dark outside yet. The good captain replied that if I didn't go to bed until it got dark, I'd have to stay up until October. Such was my introduction to the Far North's continuous daylight.

Towing the Barge Across Great Slave Lake

The cook with my pike

Then, at Hay River we were forced to tie up as a strong gale was blowing. Next morning, I took my four-month-old son nestled in a clothes basket with a mosquito bar and we went fishing. All I had for bait was a bacon rind but it had hardly hit the water when the rod was nearly pulled out of my hand. I steadily reeled the line in, all going well until my huge catch came in almost at my feet. Then it opened its ugly mouth. I dropped the rod and ran up the bank to where my youngster was in the basket. All I could think of was—alligator—and I never liked pike after that. A crew member retrieved

17

both rod and fish and later the cook made a delicious fish fry out of the seven-pound pike.

Next day we set out and traveled down-river until we came to Fort Simpson. There we dropped freight and two Mounties left us to start their new life at the Simpson Detachment. This done, we started on the last leg to our home. Two hundred miles up the fast flowing Liard River and we'd be there. Although progress was slow, all went well until we came to a small riffle in the river. It seemed such a tiny waterfall but to a loaded barge it was too much even for the diesel power. For twenty-four noisy hours the boat traveled back and forth, sideways across the river, trying to find a calm spot to move up the river. The men even used winches to try to advance the barge and boat but with no luck. Finally we tied up in a small bay and sent a radio message back to Fort Simpson to send some additional power. Two days later another freighter arrived and helped push the heavily laden barge over the riffle. Once again we were on our way.

Coming up the Liard River

Finally, on July 6, forty-two days after leaving Regina, we arrived at Fort Liard. The long journey was over and our son was a month older. After the freighter and barge were tied up to a floating dock in front of the Hudson's Bay store, Jim and I went ashore, leaving our sleeping youngster in the care of the purser. As we climbed up the path to the trail above we were surprised to see a couple waiting to greet us. They were the Hudson's Bay Factor John Forrest and his Scottish wife Bea. What a welcome they gave us! Their hospitality was genuine, partly we felt, because we were the only non-native couple they had seen in several months. The other couple who lived in the settlement, Jack and Peggy Sime, the Independent Fur Trader and his wife were out holidaying in Edmonton. We gladly accepted the Forrest's invitation to tea feeling so grateful to get off that smelly, vibrating boat but it wasn't long before the purser caught up to us, to inform us that the baby was crying. You see, he had always slept with the continuous drone of the diesel engine and didn't appreciate the sudden silence.

Later that afternoon, carrying our small son, we walked several hundred yards along the river bank to get a look at our new home. Our hearts sank a bit. It was not an impressive sight. The compound consisted of a bungalow-style dwelling surrounded by tall weeds. A large wooden warehouse stood off to one side and behind that were other large log buildings.

The house itself had not been occupied for twelve years, when it last housed two single officers. In the interim, countless generations of mice had made it their home. There was no plumbing, no electricity or running water—not even a kitchen sink. In fact, it was a shell of a house—four rooms and a path.

And so, we returned to the Bay and boarded with the Forrests while we worked on making our 'new' place livable.

First impression of our new home

Settling In

I still remember seeing our new home for the first time. What an impression it left on both of us! I didn't want to show my disappointment because it wasn't Jim's fault. He had nothing to do with the condition of the place. Maybe we were posted there because Headquarters knew what a good worker Jim was, having served on Detachment three years previously. Or maybe they didn't have another sucker who'd accept this isolated posting. Too late now! Here we were, bag-and-baggage and baby, now five months old, only three months old when we had left Regina. Really, there was nothing we could do but accept it as an adventurous challenge. The first thing, after sweeping out all the mice droppings and clearing out all the spider webs, was to install new drywall and get the walls painted. Next, we would improve the bare wood floors by covering them with heavy green battleship linoleum. So we painted—Jim, the walls in a cream color—me, I got stuck doing the trim in the same colour.

While we were working, we didn't notice a stranger who just appeared, leaning against the door frame, smoking a cigarette. He was fairly tall, probably in his late 30s, well built, and dressed in corduroy breeches and high laced leather boots and black turtleneck sweater.

"Good morning," he said. "I see you are hard at it, and it is a big improvement already. By the way, I'm Father Levesque from Fort Nelson, just down visiting the Father here at Liard," and with that he put out his hand and Jim, scrambling to get the paint off his hand, walked over and greeted our first guest. They hit it off right away.

"Say Jim, you're in good shape, I see. You must take in a lot of sports."

"Well," replied Jim, "I used to enjoy tennis, swimming and hockey—you know, the usual stuff. Besides, I was on the Musical

Ride for two years. But you look pretty skookum yourself, Father."

Father Levesque put out his cigarette (on the floor) and said, "Well, apart from my clerical duties, I do a lot of wrestling. In fact, my brother is one of Canada's top wrestlers. He works in Montreal. Say Jim, would you like a cold beer?" And with that, work ceased, but only for half an hour.

Gradually the place took shape with the addition of furniture: a Villas maple chesterfield and chairs; a Duncan Fyfe table. When I finished making the priscilla curtains and hung them up, well, things really looked better. We received a gift from an old friend and member of the Force, Havelock McLeod, who was stationed in the Eastern Arctic. It was a beautiful snow-white polar bear skin rug that contrasted nicely with the green floor linoleum, adding a splash of colour. It was tanned and finished with a half-head mount. Later, when the natives came into our house, they would carefully walk around it, or they would sit in a circle cross-legged around the rug. The four rooms slowly took on the semblance of a home. Of course, we couldn't do anything about the spaces where light shone in between the vertical boards that made the walls, letting in a fair draft. The winter's wind later emphasized that discomfort.

"I guess I'll have to requisition some insulation with next year's supplies," Jim said. "This air conditioning is a bit much." However, I must say that when the frost sparkled it made the walls look as though we had done some wild decorating.

When we first arrived at Liard, Jim was at a distinct disadvantage not being able to speak the Slavey language. Gestures worked only to a point. The Officer Commanding had stated he did not like a member to make patrols alone and notified Reid to hire a Special Constable, one who could act as a guide as well as an interpreter. Here Jim was very lucky.

The Hudson's Bay manager, John Forrest, had a chap working for him, both in the store as interpreter and as a handy man. His name was Willie MacLeod. Now Willie also ran a trap-line but because he had a regular work schedule at the Bay, he couldn't leave for any length of time to visit his traps. He was a little envious of the natives who brought in a good number of pelts while he was unable to get away. While talking to Jim one morning, Willie told him he was thinking of leaving the Bay and heading out on his own. He had a wife and three children and found it tough going on his present salary. Jim didn't say anything to Willie but approached John, the Bay manager, and asked him if he'd resent it if he offered Willie a job with the police. John, being an understanding employer as well as an efficient manager, readily agreed and Willie was duly hired as a Special Constable. Also, it was agreed that if ever John needed him in a pinch, he would help his old employer. When Jim inquired into Willie's background, Willie told him his father was a Scot and his mother was a native. He jokingly stated that he, Willie, was an 'improved' Scotsman. He soon proved to be an invaluable asset.

The next problem was to obtain sleigh dogs, not easy, since the year before we went North, distemper had gone through the area and a large number of dogs had to be destroyed. It was next-to-impossible to acquire a decent animal to help form a team. One day, three little Indian girls stopped outside our gate. They had a rather small dog, rust-red in color and he was on a tight leash. Willie, our interpreter, was just coming to work so they stopped him and asked him if the Police would shoot their dog. When asked what was wrong with it, they replied that it was lazy and wouldn't pull their toboggan loaded with wood. Willie told Jim of their request and Jim went to look at the condemned animal. As he said later, the poor animal was so thin with his coat all matted with mud, he felt it was no wonder the dog couldn't work. So he picked up the leash and told the girls he'd attend to it. Leading the submissive little mutt into the yard, Jim decided he'd not shoot it, but he'd feed him up and maybe it could help him in some way. At least it deserved a chance to prove itself.

The dog was fed small frequent meals, then Jim wormed him and put him on a regular schedule. It wasn't very long before Toby took on the appearance of a real working dog. He nearly squirmed out of his hide whenever Jim approached him. They were a great pair. Can you imagine the shock I got when I looked out the kitchen window one day and saw Jamie sitting beside Toby and the boy putting his navy tam on the dog's head? The poor dog, he just sat there, staring straight ahead but never objecting. He was alright with us but if a native came in the yard, he would get very violent, probably associating past treatment by the natives. Still, he was a great little worker and together, he and Jim pushed and pulled in quite a supply of firewood.

Later, another dog we called Fisher, who had also been sent to be destroyed was awarded the same fate and now Jim had two culls toward a team. Jim had to laugh when he took out the toboggan and harness, for both dogs would disappear into their dog houses. Gradually they realized they would not be abused and grew more co-operative.

Regular meals worked wonders. Luckily, the following season, a wonderful lead dog called Monty was flown in from Fort Norman. What an improvement he made. With a borrowed female, Jim raised his own team and they were a wonderful asset.

One dog named Rebel who was the wheel dog (the animal closest to the toboggan), and he was very smart. If he saw a rock or stump that he felt would be hit by the toboggan, he would veer away from it, not only saving the sleigh but also preventing a hard jerk to his neck. Rebel had the build of a Newfoundland dog, big and sturdy but with a shorter coat of brown and white. He was a real gentleman; some dogs would grab your hand along with whatever was offered in it but not Rebel. He would be so gentle accepting his offering. However, like most things in life, he had one fault. If he got in a fight he would have to be knocked out before he'd let go of his adversary.

Of course Jim's leader, Monty, was his favorite. Monty was no ordinary dog, but an exceptional animal with brains and a load of loyalty. Gentle and friendly, he was a well-trained American husky. Without him a team might wander aimlessly looking for a filled-in trail. If Monty went down a trail and later it became covered with deep snow, he'd crisscross till he found the old trail underneath. Without a good lead dog, the team might desert their driver and leave him stranded. He understood verbal commands immediately. Monty weighed approximately one hundred pounds, was grey in color with black points, ears erect, eyes alert. He was a much admired specimen of a working dog but he too had a drawback: that thick neck of his with the comparatively small head enabled him to slip his collar and left him free to roam.

While Jim was solving the dog problem, a new Game Warden was being appointed to Fort Liard. During the summer a house was built for him, next door to us. It would accommodate the warden, his wife and young daughter. Soon we would have a close neighbor.

One day Monty slipped the collar and went next door to the Game Warden's house. Now the Warden's wife had made a great fuss over Monty and often would pet him if they met on the trail, so he thought she was just a friend to visit. Her name was Margie. It just so happened that her little girl was celebrating her third birthday that day and Margie had baked a lovely, fancy cake. While icing it, she heard a scratching at her back door, and on investigating, she found Monty, tail wagging furiously, practically asking if he could come in. Of course, she opened the door and in he bounced, walking around the kitchen, tail wagging, just missing dishes on the table. Suddenly Margie heard her little girl calling her. The child had just awakened from her afternoon nap. "Just a minute honey, I'll pick you up." She went down the hall and lifted the youngster out of her crib. She paused to wash the little one's face then carried her out to the kitchen. Then she stopped dead in her tracks. There stood Monty, his muzzle covered with pink icing, his tail wagging him in circles. "Oh, you bad dog! Oh, you've ruined my cake. Now go, go home, go on, get!" And she opened the back door. Monty looked so pleased with himself that he almost appeared insolent as he slowly went down the steps and wandered back home, tail still wagging.

And then, there were the cats. Our woodpile was staked out by our two cats, Heather and Henry. Only thing was Heather turned out to be a Henry too. They were great pets and got along well. Only thing was that Henry, being the hunter of the two, used to watch the weasels hiding in the woodpile, and when they poked their heads out the spaces between the piled wood he would nail them, and of course, that always happened before the fur was prime. We were very careful when letting the cats out at night as a very wise old owl used to sit waiting in the tree above the back door and he was very patient. But the cats were very wary and didn't seem to give a hoot, so to speak.

Heather seemed to have a strong maternal, or maybe it was paternal instinct because, if our youngest son would wake up and cry in his crib, Heather would run into the living room where we sat and meow at us, then run back to the crib. He'd do this several times until we went with him to check out the child. We often wondered what would become of the dear little animals after we left to go 'outside.' When that time came, I hoped our replacement would have a liking for our loyal pets.

Chores

Making a home in an isolated northern community is quite different from living in the 'outside world.' Many things that had previously been taken for granted just did not exist in North.

We never used currency while in the North; if we wanted something extra, we'd charge it at the Bay or Sime's Trading store and pay the bill off each month by cheque. I remember (when we eventually returned to Ottawa) that I would always forget to take money with me when I went downtown. But it wasn't long before I wised up. I couldn't buy much with an empty purse. Most of the natives had to arrange for "jaw-bone"—a local term for credit—either with the Hudson Bay store or with the Independent Fur Trader.

One day Jim came home from the Bay store with a paper in his hand. It was a copy of a wire from Dawson Creek or City, I can't remember which. Anyway, it was to inform us that a washing machine had been shipped to us and if we didn't pick it up in ten days that we would be charged storage. Big deal! Here we were about 400 miles away, on the other side of a mountain range. The bill or notice had been sent just after our last mail and had been lying around Fort Nelson for about three months. Naturally, we disregarded the warning as the washer had been sent from the Force unknown to us, and we had no way of transporting it anyway.

Still, in the spring along came the very welcome washer, delivered by the Bay boat along with supplies for the Hudson's Bay store. Now, don't forget, at this time we didn't have electricity, but that was no problem since the washer wasn't meant to operate under electric power. It was meant for 'man' power. In the middle of the actual body of the thing was an agitator, but to activate it, one had to push-pull a handle, which was no mean matter when it was full of clothes. A wringer was attached, also to be used by two people—Jim and me. One fed the clothes into the rollers while the other cranked the handle to make them turn and wring out the water. It was hard work but certainly an improvement over the washboard and set tubs which I had to use the first two years. We worked as a team and time flew. When you enjoy someone's company, you can also enjoy the togetherness of work, and the results are twofold.

I was so glad that now it was spring, I could hang the wash on the clothesline where the wind would blow them dry instead of draping them over an improvised clothesline out in the screened-in porch where they froze stiff as a board. It was always a challenge drying flannelette sheets; they'd be so stiff and awkward when frozen that as you tried to fold them, they'd crack like a shingle bent in half. Later, I'd bring them in and put them over the kitchen chairs where they'd dry from the heat of the kitchen stove. They acted as our air freshener.

We were lucky to have that big camp stove; it heated the whole house. The only drawback was having to clean the stove pipes which were assembled in three sections. These had to be taken down, one at a time, then carried outside where they were reamed out by using a length of chain to knock out all the creosote. Creosote is caused by the burning of certain woods. It is an oily liquid which adhered to the pipes when it dried; it came from wood tar and smelled very

Washday in summer at the back door with our new washing machine strong. After the pipes were clean, they were taken back into the kitchen and reassembled for another three weeks or so. How soon depended on what I was baking for that decided the type of wood to burn. Steady heat was derived from burning maple or yellow birch. We took no chances of a build-up of creosote as a fire in the pipes could be disastrous.

We used to talk about food we missed. The other two gals were good cooks. Jim taught me how to make bread, his loaves used to rise so high. It's hard work kneading enough dough to make sixteen loaves at one time, but once it's done you don't have to do it again for at least a week. Lots of trappers made their own sourdough but I had Fleischmann® yeast in our rations so I didn't have to. One time I had the bread all ready to go into the pans when I discovered the yeast still sitting there. I had forgotten to add it. Working in that yeast was the hardest work I have ever done but it taught me a lesson I would not forget in a long time.

One chore that was a sore spot with me was this dog feeding bit. When the men went on patrol by canoe in the summer, I was left in charge of the dogs. If Jim had been assigned to the Detachment alone, he could have hired someone to feed and water them, but since he brought a wife—me—I was expected to do it, gladly, gloriously and freely, which meant "*no pay.*" I'd haul water from the rain barrels at the four corners of the dwelling house and carry it about three hundred yards to a little log building where a huge cast iron pot sat on a solid frame. And at least two trips were necessary to get enough water to mix with the dog meal. I didn't make a fire under it in the summer. If there was no water in the drums at the house, I'd have to take the yoke and two pails and get water from the fast flowing river. I still resent not getting paid, even a small tip, such as half of our fifty-cent northern allowance daily rate which was deposited directly into the bank.

An Important Announcement

After we finished the supper dishes and were sitting with some new magazines to read I said, "Hon., what would you say if I told you that Jamie's going to have a brother or sister?"

My husband practically snapped to attention although he was sitting down. "Go on, are you serious? Well, I think that's just great. There'll only be two years separating them and they can grow up together. That's a wonderful surprise, calls for a celebration. Too bad the nearest theatre is at Yellowknife."

We immediately began figuring out future plans and came to the conclusion that I should fly home to Nova Scotia on the October mail plane. Actually, I would only go as far as Edmonton on that plane, then transfer to TCA now known as Air Canada and fly East where my parents would meet me. My young son Jamie would accompany me to see his grandparents for the first time. They could spoil him and give me a break. You can see I was beginning to assume plans already and, when the July mail plane arrived, we made arrangements for me to fly out on the October mail return plane.

The summer passed and fall set in. Soon the date for the October mail was looming. I had mixed feelings about going outside because I'd have to leave Jim alone for months, but there were no facilities at the Fort to deliver a youngster and Jim was getting jumpy already.

On the 12th of October I was ready, even packed my son's little blue potty in case of an emergency. Right on schedule the mail arrived that day around 3:00 p.m. Mail arrival was the biggest event to happen to residents in the North generally but especially to us, as we received mail four times a year. The only other link to the outside was the Hudson Bay Company's wireless or the radio in winter when it was dark at night. Jim went down to the plane and helped unload the mail sacks. Then he came to the house with the pilot, Ron Cameron whom we had invited for supper. They were so solemn and quiet. I thought, hey, there's something wrong here, but right away the pilot broke the news himself.

He said, "I know you were counting on going with me on the October mail run but we discovered something that will alter your plans. When we landed, we found a broken engine mount and legally we can't take passengers or outgoing mail."

That was quite a shock. Jim persuaded the mechanic to take a note and deliver it to an old friend, Johnny Nesbitt, a pilot with the RCMP Air Division. He told him of our predicament but knew he couldn't write us back, so we had to find our own solution and hope for the best.

On our anniversary, October 17th, we packed our bags, threw in an eiderdown and loaded our big 18' freighter canoe. Jim took an extra motor, a 16 h.p. kicker just in case. We started out early in the morning up the Liard River and before long the weather turned about 20° colder. Clouds hung low over the mountains and they threatened snow. As we came around a bend in the river, we saw a scow with two trappers and their supplies. They were also headed for Fort Nelson, nearly 200 miles away. They asked us if we would like to tie alongside and travel together—you bet we would!

They arranged a tarp to keep out the wind and we got underway. The Liard River has a 15 m.p.h. current and as we were traveling against it, I felt we were hardly moving. The drone of the motors lulled Jamie to sleep so all we could do in the developing cold weather was watch for anything unusual on the banks.

Suddenly, about 3:30 in the afternoon we heard the roar of a plane flying low overhead. It dropped out of the clouds and landed alongside. It was Johnny Nesbitt and his mechanic. Quickly, my luggage was thrown up into the Norseman, Jamie was handed to the mechanic and I was very unceremoniously hauled aboard. Last thing Jim tossed up was Jamie's little blue potty. Apparently Johnny had taken the Norseman, flown directly from Edmonton to the Detachment, on finding no one there, he gassed up and took off, scanning the river to see if we were on it, and finally located us creeping along at a snail's pace.

John Nesbitt's plane the Norseman (RCMP)

Waving goodby to Jim, we took off. The weather was closing in and John was anxious to get to Peace River before dark. There was a forest fire in the area and he had to go further north to get around it, so he steam-boated that plane so low we crowded two large white birds into the spruce. I heard the two men discussing landing conditions at the Peace River and since darkness had settled in, they hoped there would be at least a car light shining on the river. However, there wasn't anything in sight as we approached the town. John said to hold Jamie down tightly as it might be a rough landing but it was so smooth a landing by the experienced bush pilot that I didn't know we had landed until Johnny cut the motor.

We found our way to the Peace River Hotel where we were to spend the night. I told Jamie who was twenty months old, "Son, you're a big boy now. No more diapers and no wet bed." From that moment on, he was housebroken. Next day we flew to Cooking Lake, Edmonton and I continued on to Nova Scotia by TCA. Johnny reported in and next day quit the Force.

I couldn't help wondering how the two men on the scow made out but later on we heard that they had been frozen in just above Nelson Forks and had to walk the remaining 140 miles to Fort Nelson. I often wondered how we would have managed.

When Jamie and I flew to Toronto via TCA, we were dressed in the same clothes in which we had started our canoe trip upriver, moose hide jacket (smoked), mukluks and mitts. We were a fragrant pair especially where it was warm. The weather was rough with lots of turbulence on the TCA flight so we had to detour and land in Milwaukee, where we reported to customs. A lot of the male passengers went to the bar and enjoyed some "good old Milwaukee beer." People stopped and stared at us in our outlandish outfits and I heard one lady say to her daughter: "Look, dear, those people are from Canada."

Then it was back on the plane and off to Toronto, where we were taken to the Royal York Hotel by limousine. My brother-in-law had been notified that we were coming and he was at the door of the hotel when we drew up. The driver unloaded our luggage and Jamie while the last article unloaded itself - Jamie's little blue potty fell out the door and rolled across the sidewalk, coming to rest at the bottom step of the Royal York Hotel. I think my bank manager brother-in-law was paralyzed with embarrassment but the door man laughingly retrieved the little pot and that broke the ice. So much for a return visit to civilization.

In due time, our new son Davie arrived in February. He was a lovely nine pounds plus baby and the nurses, one of whom would become my sister-in-law, loved to work with him. They said he was like a pre-stuffed Thanksgiving turkey: round and easy to handle.

Alternately I stayed with my parents, then with Jim's folks in Westville, Nova Scotia, until March. Then with Jamie and Davie, who was now five weeks old, we took off for our Northern home. We flew to Edmonton, then to Fort Nelson by RCAF where we took a Piper Cub run into Liard. There we were met by an exuberant team of six dogs plus a very happy husband who was delighted to say 'so long' to his batching days, and to welcome us home.

In case you're wondering about Johnny Nesbitt and what happened to him after he quit the Aviation section, well, he got a job with Eldorado and was lucky. He discovered a rich ore deposit and became a millionaire. It couldn't have happened to a nicer guy.

One thing we learned was that while we were away 'finding' the new brother, the wireless at the Bay had gone on the fritz and no messages could be received. Jim, anxious to get news about the arrival of the new family member decided to make a trip to Fort Simpson to get word there. He and Willie started out and the first half of the two hundred mile trip was quite smooth. However, the last part was new snow and Jim had to break trail for quite a distance. Arriving at Simpson, Jim was relieved and happy to hear he had a healthy nine pounds plus son so he and Willie celebrated at the Detachment, playing crib with the "boys" and trading gossip.

After two days of rest and relaxation, the men concluded the dogs were sufficiently rested and they decided to go home. They did really well for the first leg of their journey, until a storm came up and wiped out their original trail. Monty, the lead dog, wove back and forth, trying to find the packed trail underneath but the snow was too deep. Finally, Jim put on his trail shoes and broke trail for the team for a full day. Then, feeling he was starting to get snowshoe sickness, he took two strips of babiche and tied them to the front tip of his snowshoes. By pulling the tip of the snowshoe up, he managed to take a step at a time. Doing this over the miles, he finally managed to get home, but the muscles along his shins were so sore they wouldn't work for nearly a week. Shin splints, he thought, I'll never forget this trip.

Betty Reid with her two sons
Jamie and Davie

Health and Accidents

Living six years in comparative isolation, we were very fortunate to enjoy fairly good health. The nearest doctor was more than 200 miles away. There were, of course, occasional accidents and day to day minor scrapes and bruises.

In the wintertime, we put the boys outside for their nap after lunch. Well, really they weren't 'outside' exposed to the elements, just the fresh air. Jim put a toboggan out in the screened in veranda and because there weren't any glass windows, it was as cold there as it was outside, but without direct wind. Inside the toboggan, he put a four star eiderdown, then the warmly clad lads would be covered and all you could see was a little column of steam rising from the small opening. It was usually between minus 20 and –40° F. but the youngsters were as comfortable as the proverbial 'snug as a bug in a rug.' We had to awaken them or they would have slept all afternoon. They never had a cold the entire time we lived there.

When summer came (almost overnight), we slept out in the veranda as it was too hot to stay inside. Of course, like so many things, there were some disadvantages such as the sun never completely setting and those maniacal mosquitoes. Luckily the porch was well screened but the mosquitoes always managed to squeeze in somewhere and even one lone mosquito could sound as loud as a *prima donna* or a politician when it was quiet and still. So we had to erect a mosquito bar—not one they had to jump over, just squeeze through. It consisted of many yards of netting cut in a large rectangle. To the centre, we attached a strong tape, also one to each corner, then fastened the centre to the ceiling, somewhat like a canopy. The sides had to be long enough to fall in folds on the floor to keep out the pests. The children had their own mosquito bars.

The incident occurred on a sunny but cold day when I put my young son Jamie out to play. He was warmly dressed and I thought, now I can finish my baking in peace. With no one to keep him company, he wandered around in the snow pulling his little toboggan with his black and white teddy bear as the passenger and he gave it a merry ride for a few minutes. Every so often he'd call out to me, "Come on out Mom." Soon, however, his interest faded and he started to whimper so I knew he would want to come in shortly.

Suddenly this whimpering changed to a frightened cry, one of alarm. I rushed out to see if something was wrong. There he was, holding onto the top of a 45-gallon steel drum, his lower lip frozen to the top of the container. Apparently he had climbed up on the front of the toboggan to see what was in the barrel and, on leaning over, his mouth got stuck to the edge. With blood pouring down the front of his parka, I panicked. My first thought was to pull him off but something stopped me. I ran into the house and grabbed a dipper of warm water. Pouring this over his torn lip freed it up and I safely lifted him off. Although he had a sore tongue and the inside of his lower lip was ragged, it healed quickly. It must have been intuition on my part, certainly not brains because I acted instinctively. I was so grateful to some inner source that was guiding me.

There was another time, however, when our three-year-old son Jamie suddenly became ill with a very high temperature, a sore throat and could not swallow any food. Since we were two hundred miles away by canoe or dog team from the nearest doctor or hospital, we were very worried. Fortunately, the Hudson Bay Store manager had a wireless set and he sent out a message, blind, hoping someone would pick it up. We were very lucky when the RCAF at Fort Nelson picked up the call for help and the next day a plane landed on the river in front of the Detachment. It was piloted by an RCAF officer Paul Gibbs, accompanied by Dr. Vic Shearer and an aircraft mechanic. Because it was the day before Christmas, they said the real reason they responded so quickly was because of the sick child. Jamie was diagnosed as suffering from strep throat and he soon received the appropriate medicine, consisting of antibiotics to avert any serious complications.

The plane and crew then took off to return to the Airbase where their families were awaiting their return to attend a Christmas Eve party that night. Suddenly, the motor coughed and sputtered so the mechanic told Paul to look for a suitable place to put the plane down.

Seeing that the shore along the frozen river was the smoothest landing space, with skill and a bit of luck, they touched down safely.

Both the pilot and mechanic checked the engine closely and finally found the source of trouble. They looked at one another and said, "We're surely lucky that's all it is. This would be a heck of a place to spend Christmas Day. Can you imagine what our wives would say?" They took off and flew to Fort Nelson just in time to head off a search and rescue team that was getting ready to initiate a flight to locate the overdue plane. Our angels of mercy arrived home safe and sound.

There was another time when Jamie escaped what could have been a really tragic accident. He had gone with his father and dog team to the Roman Catholic Mission and he was told to stay in the toboggan while his father went in to see about buying a hunting knife. The dog team was tied to a post in front of the church. While Jim was selecting the proper knife he heard a commotion outside and looking out the window he saw the team of seven dogs in a snarling, savage fight, with Jamie down in the middle. Jim flew out and dragged the tangled mass back into an orderly line. He lifted the frightened but unharmed child to his feet. Apparently Jamie had climbed out of the toboggan, patted one of the dogs and the whole team turned around to play with him, knocking him down with the dogs fighting on top of him. Luckily he had fallen face downward in the snow and his parka had protected his head.

The dogs remembered the punishment from a length of hose and barely looked at the boy for several days.

Jim's Close Call

"Mom, where did Daddy go yesterday?", asked my son Jamie.

"Oh, he had to go and give a message to Francis Arrowhead. I imagine he'll be back later today. Would you like to carry this in for me?" And I handed him a stick of wood.

It was the next afternoon when I heard the bells of a team coming up the lane. Looking out, I saw our dog team stopping near the back door so I went out to welcome my husband and what a shock I got as I stared at him.

"Good heavens Jim," I said, "What in the world happened to your eye? It looks just awful. Oh, it's so bloody, I can't even see the pupil. Oh honey, have you lost your eye?"

The poor man didn't know if he had lost his eye or just the sight of it. He came into the kitchen and looked in the mirror.

"It does look bad, doesn't it, he said. It certainly hurt when it happened but the pain is not quite as bad now."

"How did it happen, Jim? What can we do?" I anxiously asked.

"Well," he said, "we were on the way back from Arrowhead's camp. Heading home the dogs were moving right along when a willow branch caught under the front of the toboggan and let go, springing back and hitting me in the eye. It all happened in seconds. Everything is blurred but that's because of the blood I guess."

Thankfully, the injured eye eventually healed and when we returned to Ottawa, the specialist told him he was very lucky that he had any sight at all as the scar ran right across the eyeball. Leaving it alone right after it happened was the wisest thing he could have done.

He wasn't as lucky one other time. Returning from a four-day trip in the mountains the team knew they were on the homeward trail and were moving at a fair clip. Suddenly one of the younger dogs in the middle of the team spotted a rabbit caught in a snare just off the trail and he lunged to grab it. In doing this, the toboggan swerved the slightest bit but enough to hit a rock and jolt the sleigh backward. Jim's back was given a wicked wrench and he complained of a sore back for a long time. And it was no wonder because when an x-ray was taken on our return to Ottawa, he was diagnosed as having a ruptured disc. An operation followed but because of the time lapse, the nerve had been damaged leaving him with a slight but permanent limp.

For the most part, the Slave band natives were a very healthy lot, considering the conditions under which they lived. There was an occasional case of tuberculosis, maybe caused by close contact in tents and also from the fact they neglected to change into dry clothes when they got wet. The women wouldn't go out, even on the hottest days in summer without a sweater. They didn't want their arms bare.

Even babies wore a hat and sweater in the summer time, as well as wool socks and moccasins.

Still their babies were kept fairly clean and you never heard of diaper rash. They didn't use cloth diapers. They used moss and there was a good supply of it. The moss was placed in the bottom of the back pack with the baby on top, upright of course, and then the pack was strapped to the mother's back. Sometimes the packs were made of hides but usually they were canvas and some were supported by a back board. They would travel long distances and in the spring, this is the way they returned to the settlement from the mountains after living there all winter. Their dogs were backpacked also, carrying most of the families' belongings.

When a new baby was imminent, a horizontal bar was placed waist high on top of two upright supports. The mother would lean over this bar and the baby would drop onto a clean bed of moss. It would receive the first and only bath of its life, although sometimes the young boys would swim in the river later in the summer, but the women and girls never swam.

Now it seemed the natives didn't think my husband was very reliable in predicting when a baby would arrive. One day, an anxious father-to-be paddled across the river to the Detachment and urged Jim to return with him to see why it was taking so long for his wife to deliver their baby. Jim went back with the husband to the tent where the expectant mother was leaning over the horizontal bar and thinking the event was not going to happen immediately, he told them it would be a while yet and left. The natives had the last laugh on him as the new addition was born before he got back across the river.

One day in late spring a mother arrived at the Detachment carrying a crying baby in her arms. She wanted help desperately and in those days, they always turned to the police. She brought the little one to the house and through our interpreter wanted to know what to do. We laid the baby on a blanket on our kitchen table in front of the window. Upon removing the two layers of clothes, an ugly open sore was revealed. It was red, weeping and very angry-looking, almost resembling mange. I didn't have any idea what it was and Jim was reluctant to have them stay in the kitchen since it could have been something very contagious. We had no supplies to treat such a condition, just disinfectant powder. After cleaning the wound with warm boiled water, we gave the anxious mother some sulfa powder, carefully wrapped the little one up and the mother left with her child.

Unfortunately, the baby died the next day. As far as our medical references could determine, it had a condition called scrofula. We felt totally inadequate and knowing how helpless that mother felt, we wondered what would we have done, had it been one of ours.

It seems that in summer, boats and people travel day and night in the far north since there is little darkness, what we'd call dusk. It made little difference to a traveler. Such was the case when someone pounded on our front door in the middle of the night. Jim was awakened by the loud banging and on opening the door, he was confronted by a burly deckhand holding a dirty towel around his bloody hand.

"Can you help me"? he said. "I cut my finger off."

On removing the towel, sure enough, we saw the finger was missing. My husband asked him when it had happened, and the chap said, "About an hour ago while I was coming down the river."

Jim realized that with such a short lapse of time maybe there was a chance of saving the severed finger. The two men hurried down to the boat and sure enough there lay the finger beside the offending fan belt. Luckily there was ice on board, so Jim packed the finger in crushed ice and wrapped the injured hand in clean gauze. He then sent him on his way down-river to the hospital at Fort Simpson. With the swift flowing river and the boat traveling at full speed going downstream, Jim felt the chap might get his finger sewn on in a matter of hours. The last word we heard was that the attachment had been successful.

It was a different story when a young native man met with a serious accident while chopping wood. His axe deflected off a slippery cedar log and split the top of his foot, almost up to his ankle. The cut was nearly two inches wide and several inches long. His fellow workers tried to stem the flow of blood but with little success. Fortunately an old elder heard the commotion and went over to investigate. He called to one of the natives to bring him a beaver hide and with his sharp knife he shaved a quantity of beaver hair off the pelt and packed it in the gaping cut, stemming the flow of blood.

They knew the injured lad had to be given immediate help so they made a make-shift stretcher, put him on it and carried him down to their boat. Then his two friends set out to take him to Fort Liard to seek help. Hours later they arrived at the settlement and one of the lads rushed up to the Detachment to ask for help. The police gave them gas for their motor and clean blankets for the patient. Quickly they set out for the hospital at Fort Simpson, 200 miles away.

We later heard the chap survived the trip and his foot was saved, thanks to the wise old elder and the expertise of the hospital staff. However, the nurses had quite a time getting all the beaver hairs out of the wound knowing that even one could cause infection.

The Bathtub and Other Necessities

When you turn on your water tap and you're rewarded with running water, do you ever stop to think how convenient it is? Believe me, I still appreciate it, even to this day.

Just think, I say to myself now, no melting snow, nor carrying pails of water from water barrels. Worse still or I should say better still, no walking down a steep bank with a yoke on your shoulders and two pails hanging from it so they can be filled from the fast flowing river and then staggering back up the bank with 50 pounds balanced so they would not spill all over your feet. Just turn on the tap.

Did you know there's an art to melting a quantity of snow? Maybe it's not an art but believe me, it is a method. Anyway, the first time I decided to get the wash-water ready, I put the oblong washtub on the stove. Maybe if I warmed it up, the snow would melt faster. Quickly, I emptied large pails of fresh snow into the tub and hurried to fill it to the top. All at once, the nice clean fragrance of the snow seemed to change to a burnt odor. Just then Jim came in from outside and sniffed, "What's burning? What a smell!"

I told him I wasn't cooking anything, just melting snow.

"Ye gods, woman! You're not melting it, you're burning it!"

"Don't be daft," I countered. "I'm not burning it. It's in the tub."

"Look," Jim replied, "When you melt snow, you start with a small amount and gradually add to it. It helps if you tap the side of the tub to ease the snow down into the water. No wonder the kitchen smells like the blacksmith's."

"Well," I said, "don't get your knickers in a knot. I didn't know about that. From now on, I'll let you be the snow melter."

My snow man probably realized he had come on too strong because he tempered his criticism by giving me a little squeeze and saying, "Don't feel bad, Hon. I burnt the snow in the tea kettle the first time I made tea on the trail with my Eskimo guide at Aklavik. And they didn't let me forget it!"

It was necessary to have plenty of water for nearly every night was bath night. Our youngsters loved splashing in the tub as much as the next ones, and when Jim came off patrol, a bath was his greatest reward. He was very wary he might bring home something crawly following a visit with the natives in their crowded quarters. After feeding his dogs, he'd have a hot bath before sitting down to his own supper. Usually I knew what day he'd be back and I would have it all ready with hot water from the tank next to the firebox of the big camp stove. I'd put a black bear skin on the floor and then the bath-tub could sit on something soft.

Now this bathtub consisted of a folding rectangular frame to which a heavy rubber enclosure was attached. When the frame was opened up, the tub took shape. It sounds good on paper but it was an awkward thing when it came time to empty it. You could dip out most of the water but the remainder had to be poured out the end and no matter how gently you tipped up the frame, the remaining water would rush up to the front and lots of times would run all over the floor resulting in the air turning blue from a few mild cuss words. It didn't hurt the floor which was covered with battleship linoleum but it was a lot of work cleaning up the mess. Of course, it wasn't exactly a picnic for the man of the house either as he had to carry the pails of water outside, especially when it was –40° F.

Now we just pull the plug.

The Biffy

As we sat having breakfast one morning, Jim said, "Now that we have additional help, I guess maybe our next priority (overdue to say the least) will be to replace that old outside toilet."

The additional help he referred to were the two young natives who had made a nuisance of themselves around the settlement after they got into some homebrew. The present facility had been built at least fifteen years previously by the two single officers stationed there.

Time and weather had wreaked havoc with the foundation and the little building was christened *"RICK A TEE"*. A number of cedar logs were cut and peeled immediately. I had the honor of peeling the bark, using a drawknife. A new frame was put in place, then the shiny logs formed the sides of our new "Back House".

The inside of this new addition was lined with red tin shingles which Jim had found tucked away in the warehouse. Now, wasn't that the show place, especially in winter when the temperature dropped to thirty below—then the walls of the little house would sparkle and glisten with elaborate frost patterns. Nature's expensive wallpaper, lovely! When the roof was covered with snow, it looked as though it had a coverlet resembling soft, white fur.

One lovely spring morning, when I was about to take the bread out of the oven, the back door flew open and in Jim stalked, mad as a wet hen. Taking off his old tunic, he marched into his bedroom.

"Hey, what happened—something wrong with the kids?" I asked anxiously. "Where are you going in such a rush? Is there trouble across the river?"

"Look," he said, "I'm going to the Bay. Is there anything you need?"

"Well," I retorted, squaring around to look right at him, "you don't give a person much time to decide. What's going on for Pete's sake?"

Jim paused in the middle of pulling on a clean shirt. "Look, I just happened to be in the 'john' when I heard the two boys talking outside. I heard Davie ask Jamie where Dad was. And then Jamie replied and said I was in the can, and do you know what that little three-year-old darlin' of yours said? " Let's lock the old bugger in, let him starve" So I'm going to the store to get a lock for the *inside* of that toilet door!" And with that, he was gone.

Refrigeration

"Do you know what I really miss here, so far from everything?" I asked my neighbor Bea Forrest. "I miss having an ice cream soda and having my hair done."

"Dream on," said Bea. "Without a freezer or a hairdresser, you are sunk."

Resigned to my fate, I changed my clothes and prepared to help Jim saw some birch logs. We used either a crosscut or a swede saw, one of us at either end. At first I tried too hard, and the saw balked and stuck, but after a little scolding and a lot of praise from Jim, I learned just to let the saw do the work. We cut quite a number of logs and it was wonderful exercise. I had the muscles to prove it. Luckily, I didn't have to split the wood.

Finally, Jim acquired a couple of prisoners, thank goodness, and now the work could be split up—no pun intended. One chap had bought a can of malt and brewed a batch of beer for it was legal to buy the malt and sugar and hops at the traders' stores. Of course, he made the beer one day and drank it the next. And got loaded! He threw all the furniture and pots and cooking utensils out of his cabin and was generally obnoxious to all of his friends. So they complained and the poor chap got hustled off to jail. Of course, the definition of jail was Jim's office. No other facility was available. It was directly behind our dwelling house and was made of logs. There he sobered up and after breakfast the next day, Jim announced the work order for the day. It was to build an ice house.

Because of the permafrost, the ice house

The prisoner leaving with his newly acquired possessions after finishing the ice house.

would have to be built underground. Jim, Willie and Vallee, the prisoner, dug down ten feet making a square hole. One man would stay in the hole and fill the pails which in turn, were hauled up with ropes. Finally, when it was empty of earth, they lowered logs down and formed four walls, lining the spaces between the logs with moss, chinks packed tightly to make them airtight. Next, a ladder was attached to one wall, allowing a person to go down to the floor and a heavy wooden cover finished the 'ice house,' keeping out the elements.

In the late fall and early winter, the men took crosscut saws and cut ice blocks from the river, hauling them by dog-team to fill the ice house. These blocks lasted through to the next summer and were very welcome! It was very hot during the summer—well above 90° Fahrenheit—and a drink of ice water was very refreshing. I would make Jell-O and it actually set in the summer; you can imagine how popular I was. I made the stuff for anyone who could find a package of it. We tried to make ice cream with Jack Sime's ice cream maker but, although everyone took turns cranking the thing, after half a day, we finally quit and gave the ingredients to the dogs.

First Hair Cut

"Look, my boy," I scolded Jim. "You need a haircut. Soon you'll look like Buffalo Bill." Actually I was grossly exaggerating because it wasn't anything quite that bad, as Jim always kept his hair short. He'd look really silly if for some reason he suddenly had to appear in his Stetson, so he admitted it was long and since we had been supplied with clippers, manual ones, maybe I could take a stab at it. I thought to myself, good choice of words.

He sat straddled on a chair facing the back of it so I could get closer to the back of his head. First I combed his hair, then went around a couple of cowlicks to find a part. I started clipping down at the neck, then went up the back of his head a-ways. He never told me that you're supposed to release the handles when you wanted to stop so I just stopped and pulled the clippers back. You should have been there. You'd think a bag of cats had got at it. The air was blue. I never knew he could talk like that but I did see a big clump of blond hair

45

Jim's first haircut

still caught in the razor. There weren't any roots visible on the blade so I wasn't too concerned, but to put it mildly, I knew he was annoyed.

He had a mirror in each hand so he could monitor progress in the back but that made me very nervous. My hands were so sweaty I kept dropping the comb. He conceded it was only a week between a good and a bad haircut. Still, he did look a little moth-eaten at the back. Too bad, because I was the only 'good' barber in town. Years later when we returned outside and lived in Ottawa, I was very much surprised that my haircutting skills hadn't improved that much. There was an official opening which he had to attend and at the last minute he asked me if I could trim his hair—this time he had electric clippers.

I got halfway up his head when the clippers broke, actually broke. He jumped up, whipped off the cloth from around his neck and tore out the door. He drove straight to the barber shop which kindly let him in two minutes before six o'clock. Jim said, "Can you give me a trim? My wife started but the clippers broke."

"It's a good thing!" exclaimed the barber.

Electricity

Do you remember the times when your hydro suddenly went off? Left you in the dark scrambling for that fancy candle you were saving, or that flashlight that was never in the same place twice. Well, after three o'clock each winter's day our source of light, the sun, was cut off by the Arctic night.

The first year we used coal-oil lamps, the kind with wicks and chimneys that got all smoked up and smelly. The next year we graduated to Coleman lanterns, but I was always nervous about lighting them, as they sometimes flared up. But they supplied instant heat when Jim had to get up in the middle of the night to warm up a baby's bottle.

We had an annual inspection by the Officer Commanding from Ottawa and while he was there, we inquired into the possibility of being supplied with a wind-

Jim Reid installing the windcharger

charger. We were told it was highly improbable.

The next year he was back and I was still struggling with lanterns; I asked the Officer Commanding if it would be alright if my father sent in a wind-charger as a Christmas gift because he too was concerned about a fire hazard. Although we received a noncommital reply, lo and behold! Next summer a wind-charger arrived. Ours was a small bluff born of desperation but it worked.

With the arrival of the wind-charger on the same freighter as our annual supplies, the men were faced with the task of erecting the equipment. After making a cement base, the seventy foot high frame was erected. The charger had a propeller on top. When the wind blew too hard the prop would stand up on end, acting as a brake; when the wind abated it would return to its vertical position. It was connected

47

to a bank of batteries which were installed in the little cellar nestled under the kitchen (where we also kept our canned goods.)

The wind provided the energy to charge the batteries which in turn supplied the source of electricity for our radio and lights. Now after three o'clock or thereabouts, we would not be denied light previously supplied by the sun or the primitive lamps. We had gone modern! So when you turn on that light switch today, reflect how far we've come and give some thought to saving some of that energy for future generations.

The Garden Attempt

It was a cold winter's night with the rafters snapping from the cold like a shotgun going off, when all of a sudden, our back door flew open and Jack Sime, our Independent Trader friend, rushed in quickly shutting the door behind him.

"Do you know it's frosty out there tonight? My thermometer registered 46 below when I left home. Halfway here, I was wishing I was already back." And with that Jack pulled off his toque, parka and mitts, and wrung his hands over our welcome, warm camp stove.

"Is anything wrong, coming out in this weather?" I asked, now just a bit worried that he had something urgent or even worse, bad news, to tell us.

"Oh no, nothing like that, but the wife was writing letters and reading the various magazines when she came across the seed catalogue, so I thought I'd take a break. By the way, do you realize you'll have to order your seeds for the next mail plane, otherwise it'll be too late—about five months too late?"

Gosh, we'd never thought of that. "I guess we'd better get an order ready. A good thing you're on the ball. We certainly want to plant a garden. Now, how about a hot chocolate to warm you up?"

Jack's smile was his consent.

After he had finished his hot drink, Jack left and Jim and I had a great discussion on what we should plant and what seeds we should order. I started with the idea that we should have tall flowers in the front of the house and some shorter plants for window boxes.

"Hold it, hold it!" My husband squared around and facing me

48

Our Garden

head on, stated, "We can't eat flowers, short or tall, so vegetables should be our top priority. If we have room, we'll include some of your favorite flowers. Let's make a chart where things are to be planted and take it from there. Personally, I favour sweet peas."

"Well," I countered, "we can't eat sweet peas but they could be classified as 'tall plants.' " One point for me. And with that I let the subject drop.

Both Jim and I were brought up by parents who inspired us to take an interest in gardening and now, living so far from a supply of fresh foods made it imperative we plant a variety of vegetables.

In the North, the month of April meant spring and it arrived overnight with the impetuous haste of a voluptuous land suddenly freed from a frozen girdle. First the river ice in front of the house rotted, eventually breaking up into massive, grinding ice floes. These would roll huge rocks along and could grind full-grown trees to splintered shards that floated down-river like overblown matchsticks. The power of rushing ice is awesome.

The first day of May was warm, the sun shone for nearly the full day and nature burst forth in all her glory. Leaves clambered out of their buds, the dandelions rushed up to present a yellow welcome and the birds returned, adding music to relieve the chattering of squirrels. Finally the sun was warm! All this translated into one word. Spring? No...work! The garden had to be dug over—no rototillers in those days, just a shovel, a delving fork, a rake and two strong backs: his and mine.

The first crop planted was potatoes on May 24th, with smaller seeds soon following. Our garden was a good size, probably 150 feet in length, extending from the front of the house right to the fence in front of the river. As we prepared the soil, I said, "I don't see any earth worms here. I read somewhere the plants won't grow well without earthworms to work the ground."

Jim explained that under this surface layer of soil lay the permafrost which never melted, so worms and snakes couldn't survive. That was great for me. I didn't worry too much about bears or wolves but I'd walk half a mile out of my way to avoid meeting a snake. Big earthworms didn't exactly thrill me either.

Do you know that when we first ordered potato seed I thought we'd get at least a quarter of a potato as seed? Do you know what we received in the mail from the seed place? Well, we got eyes. Little dugout eyes, there must have been one hundred to a box. I was amazed, no, I think I was fractured; they sent us eyes to plant and expected potatoes from such a tiny thing. I was so upset I didn't say a word and it's a good job I didn't, because on July 6, we dug the first potatoes. Once more I realized I had a lot to learn. Is it possible I was a slow learner?

Jim erected chicken wire between two posts so he could plant his favorite sweet peas. He never guessed they would reach over six feet and be so delightfully fragrant. It wasn't the fragrance of the flowers that attracted the native women to come right into the yard but the many different colors. The women came in pairs, never alone, and they admired the varied hues, talking excitedly among themselves, pointing to the reds and yellows, exclaiming over the different colors. I imagined that they had discussed how to copy them and blend them on their own beautiful silk works; what plants and berries would effect the dyes they needed to produce the colors nature had brought forth. I wished I could have understood their language so that I too could have appreciated their enthusiasm.

Every night around eleven o'clock we were blessed with a heavy rain shower that lasted for nearly half an hour and then the sun returned for a new sparkling day. The plants just shot up. The garden produced huge cabbages and a great abundance of carrots. Jim filled a 45-gallon drum with sand and stored it in the little cellar under the kitchen covering layers of carrots with the sand. They kept well although retrieving them was hard on the fingernails. When I got near the bottom of the barrel I had to be careful as I was short on one end and could go head first into the deep drum. The large eight-pound cabbages, turnips and beets were also stored in the little cold cellar room.

We were careful to keep the cellar door closed so that Jamie, our son, couldn't go down there since that was also where we stored our year's supply of canned goods. We didn't want an episode similar to the one that happened to a family at Nelson Forks. One day their little fellow strayed into their unlocked storage and peeled off all the labels from cases of fruit and vegetables. The poor cook always had to shake the cans before opening and even then it was a 50:50 chance, strictly a "Guess what we're having for supper."

Fresh Food

How we loved getting fresh meat! After eating very salty, boiled dinner or canned sausages for three or four months - anything fresh had great appeal. Even the vegetable supply was dehydrated and the best of that was dried cabbage. We made up instant potatoes, mixed in a can of corned beef and added reconstituted cabbage—suddenly you had conceived a real Jigg's dinner.

Once I roasted a beaver. We ate it cold but it was a bit stringy. Another time, the purser off the Hudson Bay boat gave us a very relished piece of caribou. What a gift—much like beef tenderloin! It didn't provide you with ample extended energy, but like fresh moose meat, it was a grand treat.

Of course, there was a bountiful supply of fish. In a lake about forty miles away were lake trout weighing forty or fifty pounds. However, these giants had a very strong flavor and the natives used them for dog food.

Partridge, willow grouse and prairie hens were also plentiful. The hens used to land on the top of the house, all lined up. Peg and I would take our .22 rifles and go out the Hay Lake trail hunting partridge as we weren't keen on prairie hens. Together we got twelve one day. They were heavy to carry home so we dug up some roots and carried them slung between us.

When I showed my share to Jim, I said: "I bring them—you clean them—I cook them."

"Good arrangement, I'd say," agreed Jim. Poor Peg, she had to clean her own birds. Jack said they'd make him sick. Eating them didn't seem to bother him too much, however.

In the fall of our third year, we were very fortunate to receive a hind quarter of moose meat. A native brought this in from the mountains and Jim happily swapped tins of canned meat for it. The natives liked the ribs and large bones of the moose much more than the meaty quarter. They would roast them on their open camp fires, then crack the bones open and eat the marrow. What we considered the choice cuts, big steaks or roasts, they fed to their dogs.

The weather was still quite warm so we had to protect the meat from hordes of flies, not to mention other interested animals. Jim took the large cut of meat and hung it up near the top of the windcharger where it would be safe. Because of the height, no flies could reach it. The strong sun and wind dried a heavy casing around the meat - nature's way of preservation. When we needed fresh meat, Jim climbed up the charger ladder and cut some off. We felt very fortunate for these meals and the native fellow had a reserve supply of canned food if game was scarce while on his trap line.

After freeze-up late in the fall, a large native family with a complement of small children and a pack of dogs arrived at the settlement. They had walked forty miles from Trout Lake to stock up on supplies before setting off for their winter trap lines. They obtained a quantity of flour, tea, matches, salt and maybe a toy for the younger ones. The women picked out the brightest colored duffel cloth to make liners for their mukluks or moccasins and fine cloth for parkas and trim. With all their purchases recorded and piled together, the men then congregated to talk and smoke with the rest of the group. The women and children stood by patiently until told to pack the dogs and get ready to leave, the dog packs averaging around forty pounds.

Jim with his Special Constable Willie had an incident which began with a visit to the Hudson Bay store. Francis Arrowhead, the Chief of his camp, told Willie a story about his most recent moose hunt. While making camp, he had pitched his tent in a nice sheltered spot. During the night he awakened to a steady, low noise that seemed to be coming from just outside the tent. Deciding to investigate in the morning, he went back to sleep. Imagine his surprise when he discovered he had slept on top of a bear den. The group listening to his story thought this was a great joke—a snoring bear!

Jim and Willie returned home discussing what they would have done if they had discovered the sleeping bear. Right then and there they decided to go and check out the camping spot. Harnessing the two dog teams, Jim and Willie took off to locate the area Francis had described. It wasn't long before they approached the sheltered spruce stand. They tied their teams, then approached the side of the hill. Ahead of them, a small column of vapor escaped from a frost-encircled opening.

Jim pointed, "Here's the den." Kneeling, they listened for any sounds from within the den. They heard a soft, rumbling noise and knew they had found the sleeping bear.

Willie said, "Let's wake him up." He cut a long pole and sharpened one end. Inching the stick down through the narrow den opening, he twisted it and pulled it back up. A clump of black hair clung to the end; sure enough there was a black bear asleep in a den below. He poked and twisted several more times, each time retrieving another small clump of dense black hair. Finally the bear had enough and with a roar he charged up from his winter quarters. Willie took careful aim and shot him. Enlarging the entrance to the den the two men dragged the bear out. Between them, they loaded the bear on the toboggan and brought him home. The skinned-out carcass was divided equally but I got the best deal—suet for the Thanksgiving pudding and the dense hide for gleaming black bearskin mitts.

One day in mid-winter the Royal Canadian Air Force from Fort Nelson radioed the Bay that they would be making a routine flight to put in required hours, and would we like some fresh eggs? No indecision there. So down they came, landing on the frozen river in front of the Detachment. Jim quickly harnessed the team and went down to meet them. The precious cargo was placed in the toboggan and hauled up to the front door of our house. Jim went to the side of the sleigh and bent over to take out the case, but Squadron Leader Paul Gibbs said, "Just a minute, Jim, let me do that." And he reached in to lift out the case of eggs. As he did, the bottom of the case gave way and thirty dozen eggs cascaded down the front of his uniform and broke on the snow.

There was nothing anyone could do so Jim just turned the team around and the dogs gladly and quickly cleaned up the mess. I thought to myself "Oh no! Not those awful powdered eggs again." Of course, I had to resort to them until our annual ration of two cases of eggs arrived on the supply boat in the summer. Jim used to turn the flats of eggs over each month so that the yolks wouldn't settle but even so I was careful using eggs when baking.

Did you ever have an egg explode? You'll need more than fresh air. In those days a Northern Cook never broke an egg directly into the mixing bowl. It was always cracked into a saucer, just in case.

Native Ways

One never heard of much violent behaviour among the Northern natives. Their survival and well-being depended on mutual respect and support. However, brew was the catalyst for many disagreements and most times that took place between husband and wife.

You might wonder where the intoxicant came from? Well, to begin with, both stores—the Hudson's Bay and the Independent Fur Trader— sold the ingredients legally; they were contained in one can labeled *John Bull's Malt.* If a native was fortunate enough to own or borrow a crock, it was used. If not, then any large pot would do. In would go the malt, then the required amount of hot water and, if they wanted an additional kick, they would add raisins to speed the fermentation. Now, wait a couple of days and, voila! They produced a brew which could only be described as 'Northern Sunshine'! Why was malt supplied to the stores? Well, originally, it was supposed to be used in making bread, but it was easier and more pleasant to drink the result than to bother baking it. Imagination played a large part in the success of the product. It seems they thought they were inebriated by just smelling the fumes.

One incident, more comical than tragic, occurred one late afternoon when a native came to the detachment, very distraught. In fact, he was close to tears. He told Jim his wife was very mad at him because he had drunk too much of his latest batch of brew and she had thrown him out of their house. Following him out were all his belongings and finally their little camp stove. Alexi wanted sympathy but didn't find it in Jim's office. He wanted Jim to return home with him and talk to his wife. Taking the husband back across the river to his shack, they found everything out in the yard and an irate wife guarding the door with a broom in one hand and a big willow switch in the other. In broken English she told her husband to "Get out and stay out until he was sober."

The disappointed husband was escorted back to the Detachment where he was told to sleep it off before returning home.

We were careful not to assault the native customs or beliefs. After all, they didn't need us to survive since they had been there long before us. Our job was to remind them that they too had limitations and laws that everyone should abide by.

We were very interested and often quite amazed at the way the young native children obeyed their parents and

Alexi with the cowboy hat

respected them. Sometimes a glance was enough, no scolding necessary. The older natives believed that young minds were controlled by the more powerful minds of the parents, as they were their first teachers. They, in turn, had been taught by the Great Spirit. Their belief was that the child's mind was empty and open when it was born—free of bad attitudes—and it was up to parents to protect them. They felt all this should happen in the first seven or eight years and then the youngsters would remember their lessons for life.

The Autopsy

It was one day in February, when Jim and his hired man Willie were away on a routine patrol, that two native chaps came across the river to the Detachment. They said they had brought in a young man who had been murdered in the mountains, and they had left him in his widowed mother's tent.

His body had been placed beside a small camp stove which supplied heat for the living quarters, and the mother, very upset and saddened, had sent word over to the police that she wanted to see them right away. Through the messenger, I sent word that the police were out on patrol but she replied that I should go and see her but to come quickly.

The two men took me across the river to the camp by dog team where I was led to the mother's tent. As well as I could, I tried to tell her how sorry I was and asked if I could do any thing to help her. She said she just wanted the police to see the boy and to see the boy's nails, which had a bluish hue. She thought too that he had marks on his neck. I couldn't see any marks of violence but I didn't make any comments about the condition of the body. I did suggest, however, that she have the lad's body transferred over to the mission, out of that very warm tent.

On inquiring two days later if the body had been moved, I was informed she hadn't transferred him. I sent word over the river that if an investigation was to be held, it would have to be done at the Roman Catholic Mission where there was room. She complied finally, and the remains were placed in a separate building on church property. At the time I fleetingly wondered why he was placed in a shed instead of in the actual church, but later realized that if he had been placed in the church, the natives would never have gone in there again.

A very strong belief was woven in their culture; the mystery of death was feared but respected. When one of their members died, all his or her possessions were destroyed, often their sleigh dogs were shot, and their harness thrown up in the trees. Dishes and pots were either buried or burned. We were surprised to learn that if a person died and left money in the vault at the Hudson Bay store, the surviving family wouldn't touch it and it was left there. What eventually happened to it was never discussed or revealed. Their belief was so strong that if a person was expected to die, that individual was moved out into a tent, thus saving the house from destruction.

A tent was less valuable and easily replaced.

Jim came back off patrol at the end of the week and was soon made aware of everything that had happened. Immediately, he radioed Fort Simpson and contacted the doctor who was also the Indian agent and coroner. The good doctor sent back word that he had previous commitments but as soon as weather permitted and a plane available, he would fly into Fort Liard.

It was nearly six weeks before Doctor Truesdale finally flew in. He came directly to the Detachment to pick up Jim, to go with him to perform the autopsy, and determine if there was any foul play. The Indians had heard so many stories that the lad had been murdered during a brew-drinking party that Jim wanted a medical report from the Indian agent.

The doctor asked me if I would go along as witness to the procedure. I readily agreed and we set off on our walk to the Mission. On the way, Dr. Truesdale said he would like to drop into the Bay store and pick up a new skinning knife which he could use. We continued our way through the willow trail and came out at the Roman Catholic Mission where the autopsy was to take place in a former hen house. It should be noted that during the lapse of time when the chap's body was brought in from the mountains to the time of the actual autopsy, some warm chinook winds had passed through and the body had thawed and frozen several times.

Dr. Truesdale made a "T" incision on the chest and lifted the breast bone up. When he checked the lungs, the lobe of the right lung was full of ice crystals and the doctor said he had died of double pneumonia. The intestines were dotted with many T.B. tubers, a condition, our medical friend informed us, that was alarmingly prevalent among a high percentage of natives. Digging around he said, "And here's the appendix," but a few seconds later he corrected himself and said, "Oh no, here's the appendix over here." Both Jim and I glanced sideways at each other, secretly glad it wasn't an operation on either one of us. Next the doctor punctured the stomach to see what his last meal consisted of and the resulting horrendous odor that assaulted us made the doctor act quickly. The body was hurriedly stitched up and carefully wrapped in a clean white sheet,

58

preparatory for burial. The mother later expressed relief knowing her boy had not met with foul play.

Before we left for the mission, I had put a roast of mountain sheep in the oven. On opening the kitchen door, suddenly we were assailed with the same offensive odor we had just experienced a few minutes before. Unanimously, we agreed the roast had been bad and it was dispatched to the dog pot forthwith. Our parkas and mitts were hung outside and everyone took turns scrubbing hands and brushing teeth. Then we settled down to the old standby: canned sausages, dehydrated cabbage and dried potato flakes.

The next day a funeral service was held in the quiet little cemetery behind the mission, attended by a few friends and the boy's best friend, his mother.

Willie

One midwinter's day, the weather was cold but clear with the temperature at −20° Fahrenheit. Jim and Willie decided to make a routine trip to a native camp about ninety miles away. Together they packed their toboggans, taking bannock, beans and some canned meat. Dog food made up the remainder of the load. They agreed to leave the following morning after breakfast.

Next day, Jim laid out his harness for the team, done in the tandem style because the trails would be narrow. Then he went to get his leader, Monty, because he always put the lead dog in the harness first to keep the traces taut. Well, when Jim went to get the leader, the big dog was nowhere to be seen. His collar lay empty in the snow. Jim whistled and called but no answering bark came from the dog. Surely he wouldn't have gone visiting dogs in the settlement, Jim thought, because things were very quiet. If a loose dog was about, there would be a great ruckus from the other tied dogs.

Suddenly Jim remembered the trap he had set out on the back trail behind the dog houses. A large timber wolf had been prowling in that area and sleigh dogs were too precious to be maimed or killed. With a sense of foreboding, Jim rounded the bend in the trail and was shocked to see his lead dog caught by his front paw in the steel jaws of the number three trap. Quickly, he opened the trap and released

Monty's foot. It was frozen solid. He led the limping dog back to the warehouse and put him inside while he went to get help from his partner. Together they discussed the situation and naturally, the planned trip was cancelled. But the immediate problem was what to do for the dog. His paw did not appear to be broken but he might lose it because of frost bite. Likely gangrene would set in.

In the back of Jim's mind, he remembered a story a trapper had once told him when the same thing had happened to one of his dogs. He told Jim that he took coal oil and put the paw in it. Jim decided to try it. The two men warmed some coal oil just enough to take the frost out of it. Then they put the paw in the solution and held it there for several minutes. The howls of pain were deafening when the frost started coming out of the frozen paw, but gradually the circulation was restored. The pain eased and the paw was gently dried off. The dog limped back to his house where he curled up in the snow to rest after his all night ordeal. After two days rest, Monty was back to his old form. The pad on his foot didn't even show a crack.

Three days passed and after a good snowfall, Jim and Willie decided to make the postponed trip. On the way, Willie checked one of his traps that had been set out a few days earlier. In one of his number four traps, he found a dead wolf, frozen. He was going to dispose of it but Jim said he would like to have it for the hide. So they loaded it onto Jim's toboggan and continued on their way.

On approaching the camp, Willie told Jim to cover the wolf up well as the natives would be very upset to have a wolf, even a dead one, in their camp. They believed that in killing a wolf, they would be killing the spirit of their grandmother and their rifle would never again shoot straight. So the carcass was completely hidden under a tarp.

When the men arrived, it was time for the evening meal. The natives were cooking a large whitefish and they invited Jim and Willie to sit with them. The men gladly accepted the offer since having to eat half- frozen canned food after a long day traveling wasn't too appealing. Jim offered them canned meat in exchange for warm fish. Willie, watching closely, told him to make sure they didn't spot the hidden wolf or they wouldn't touch the cans of supplies. All went well. The men thoroughly enjoyed the fresh fish which had been cooked, innards and all, and the natives were delighted to get the canned goods in exchange.

On their way home one of Willie's dogs played out and both teams stopped for a rest. Jim and Willie walked over to a tall spruce tree and Jim proceeded to cut off some 'gum' which oozed from the bark. It looked like balsam or resin.

"Do you like that stuff, Jim? I'd much rather have cut plug chewing tobacco. Don't you find that stuff takes a long time to soften up?"

"Oh, it's not so bad," replied Jim. "It's a good substitute when you can't get real gum. The boys don't care for it tho'. And that chewing tobacco, well once I tried it and I must have swallowed some because in short order I felt like I was up in the clouds. I'd never touch that stuff again."

"I noticed Emerence coming out of your place yesterday. Everything all right with her and Joe?" Willie asked.

"Oh yes," replied Jim. "They're getting along better now that they have the place to themselves. His sister was a bad influence and it's just as well Joe shipped her out." He straightened up after tying the snowshoe to the backboard of his toboggan. "You should have been there, Willie. I had a big operation to perform on Emerence."

Willie's ears perked up, his curiosity showing. Not to keep him in suspense or encourage his imagination, Jim proceeded to tell him the following story of what happened so that rumors wouldn't get started.

"Emerence came to the house with a sore arm. Something hard was stuck under the skin of her upper arm. It was too big to be a thorn, maybe it was a splinter, and it was really bothering her so she wanted me to cut it out.

I told her I didn't have a scalpel nor a really sharp small knife but if she wasn't nervous I could use a razor blade. She said she wasn't afraid so I got a razor blade, put a pan of water on the stove, brought it to the boil and dropped in the blade. After it had boiled hard for five minutes, I took it out and when it was cool enough to handle I started to operate. Well, not really operate. I just had to cut the skin.

Well, let me tell you something, Willie, I never knew the human skin could be so tough. Twice I tried to cut above the embedded thing and twice I couldn't get through. I was more nervous than she was. I felt sort of weird trying to cut human skin. Finally I pressed on the bottom of the embedded object and at the same time I cut across the top of it and the darn thing just popped out. It was a porcupine quill. I poured peroxide on the cut; it foamed up, stinging a little but good old stoic Emerence, she just smiled. I put a little gauze on it; she rolled her sleeve down, looked at me and said, 'masse cho' (which means thank you much) and off she went. I was glad she hadn't swallowed it.

Jim said he was glad he wasn't home when Jack Sime came to get him. Joe Donta's wife was having a miscarriage and she sent for the police. My wife told him I was away so he said for her to come and help. She told him she had no experience with those things but Jack insisted she accompany him back to Donta's cabin. Apparently she took some clean cotton and safety pins and away they went but by the time my wife arrived it had all happened, so she wrapped up the expelled fetus and dropped it down the outside 'john.' My wife told Mrs. Donta to take it easy for a few days. Next day she took a loaf of newly baked bread and away she went to check on her patient. When she walked into the yard, beside the cabin there was Mrs. Donta scrubbing on the washboard, right as rain. What could she say? These people knew their own limitations, so you don't interfere with their customs."

Tea and Other Parties

"Is there anything you need from Sime's store?" Jim asked. "I have to go up and stamp some hides for Jack this afternoon. He thought there might be a chap passing through picking up cleared fur to take out to Edmonton. I told him I'd help him bale the skins."

"No, nothing unless you'd ask Peg if I could borrow the latest catalogue from Eatons. You didn't happen to take mine over to the office by any chance, did you?"

"Nope, I haven't seen it lately," replied Jim. "It'll likely turn up where you least expect it."

Right, I thought, it's likely out in the Biffy where the last one wound up—taken by a certain individual who wanted to look up the price of fishing tackle, stuff like that.

When Jim finally came in for supper, he put Peg's catalogue on the table and chatted away while I poured a hot cup of tea for him.

"I saw Ed Cooper up at Jack's. He's a good worker, that chap, responsible too. He had his wife Theresa with him and two of his youngsters. Peg wants you to go up to tea tomorrow, I think Bea Forrest is going too. Oh, by the way Ed offered me a dog he doesn't want, says it's lazy. I didn't say I'd take it, we'll see, that's one thing I don't need, an animal holding the rest back."

Next day I met up with Bea and we walked up to Simes' for our 'tea party.' It was fun getting dressed up once in awhile. Made a husband sort of sparkle too! When we got to Peg's we met Theresa Cooper and two of her little ones. Theresa was a very attractive native girl and her children were clean and well dressed. She had beautiful moccasins of which I was especially envious.

We had quite an afternoon, Theresa saying she had been busy berry picking. Bea asked her if she always took her children with her when she went to the barren lands for berries. "Oh no," Theresa replied, "I find someone to look after them then. I've heard so many stories of natives who set their babies down while they picked berries and if the babies cried, the bears would come and carry them off."

We didn't have that problem where we lived, no berries there.

A Different Tea Party

A Geodesic survey team made its home base at Liard for a short time one summer. Geodesy is the science that deals with methods to determine the size, shape, curvature and area of the earth. The group was under the supervision of Mr. Ney from Ottawa. The survey team had their work cut out for them because of the rugged terrain, fast flowing rivers and flies. Lots of flies: mosquitoes, black flies, blue flies and deer flies. Mr. Ney, being from Ottawa was a most welcome visitor as we were familiar with the area and enjoyed his company at dinner occasionally. He was so interesting and dedicated to his work, it was obvious why he had been awarded the Order of the British Empire.

Over coffee after dinner one evening, Mr Ney and Jim were discussing and predicting the future of Canada with its untapped wealth of minerals and gas deposits still lying undiscovered in the far North. Jim then told him of a personal experience he had and it wasn't very far from our settlement.

He and Willie were returning from a visit to some outlying natives. They stopped to make tea and didn't like the look of the muddy water in the creek. Jim scraped the deep moss aside to see if he could get water underneath. He found none but oil oozed up to the surface.

"Well, look at that!" exclaimed Jim. "There's more of that oil the natives were complaining about. I guess we might as well wait until we get home for that tea."

Relaying the story to our guest, Jim was quite unprepared for the interest he showed and even more so when the man encouraged him to contact Imperial Oil in Edmonton and advise them of his finding. He did so but the company informed Jim his discovery was too isolated to justify any investigation but years later we heard that different oil companies were drilling in that area.

When we returned to Ottawa, we were invited to tea at the home of Mr. and Mrs. Ney who lived on the Ottawa River. Gladly we accepted their invitation. However, (there always seems to be a 'however' in our life), we were obliged to bring along our two older boys, one nearly three years old, the other four and a half. This was their first exposure to precious ornaments and antiques. They were as wild as proverbial March hares; excited being in such a large home, they took off their shoes and slid on the hardwood floors from one end of the room to the other. What one missed, the other made up for it. But the crowning caper was when they tried to climb up inside the fireplace. I was mortified. Jim was livid. Muttering apologies, he took both boys by the collar and marched them to the door.

Mrs. Ney appeared justifiably relieved but she graciously expressed her feelings, saying: "Now you must come again some time when you can get a sitter."

Fun and Games

Although wolves were often heard to howl in the high country, Saturday night was our time to have fun. We would alternate going to the other houses (there were only three altogether). After the Game Warden's house was built next door to us, then there were four. We all knew how to play cribbage and had some wild games, playing with someone else's husband as a partner. Also we played a lot of Rummoli, but not for money. I think we used chips, no one carried cash with them in those days. Sometimes, if it was during the hockey finals, the men would balk in the middle of a card game, especially if they were losing.

If we went up to Sime's, the Independent Fur Trader's house, Jim would put the eiderdown in the carryall and hook up four dogs. The two boys sat in front of me and away we'd go, up the trail to our friends. Jim ran behind most of the time. We thought we were pretty lucky.

Bill King and Andy Jensen were invited also. I think they went along mainly for the lunch served afterwards. They were lots of fun. Everyone got along well together, you had to and the time passed quickly.

On Friday nights, there was a program broadcast from Edmonton called "The Northern Messenger." It was on the CBC, and everything stopped for that. Folks from the *outside* sent messages to be read to the Northerners, and if you were lucky, you would hear your name and news. Lots of times the Northern lights would dance in the heavens and interrupt transmission at the crucial part of a message. Of course, the program wasn't aired in the summer as it was daylight all night. The radio required darkness in those days.

Spring and fall were a time of utter isolation, completely cut off from the outside world until the river cleared and ran free. We had to rely upon our own ingenuity for entertainment. Every Wednesday, if the weather permitted, the other two women and I would get dressed up, which meant shoes and stockings, and a skirt or dress, and we'd go to each other's house, alternating each week. The hardest part was to think up a new or different dessert. All three of us had the same ingredients so it really depended on our imaginations.

I made up my mind to accomplish three things during the winter wait: learn to play bridge; to read the whole Bible; and finally to learn how how to turn the heel of a sock. My experiences with learning to play bridge were varied but for the most part a staggering success. My worst encounter was a reply to a demand bid.

I attempted to read the whole Bible several times. Some parts were very familiar. Others suggested a need for rationalization. After several starts throughout six years, I wasn't exactly quotable. Mostly 'do's' and 'don't's.' I still think the golden rule should be universally stressed. I thought that would be the fairest solution to many different problems.

My final resolution: the sock. Although I had survived a successful career on staff of an Eastern university, I discovered it was next too impossible to get the starting stitches to remain on a knitting needle. Eventually, I did make a pair of socks for my father with a beautiful maple leaf adorning each instep. I learned later from my mother he couldn't wear them. They were so loose that they kept disappearing down into his shoes. I made up my mind to ask one of the women to teach me how to knit.

Betty with a team of pups

The Scarlet Scarf

My neighbor, Bea Forrest was an accomplished knitter. Often when she dropped in, she'd bring her work with her. Truly, I admired her ability to smoke and talk and knit all at the same time. And her resulting handiwork was to be admired, at least by me. Taking mental stock of my attributes, I knew I could never enumerate them as there would be too many blank spaces.

Finally, one day I swallowed my pride and asked Bea if she'd teach me to knit, just get me started. Being a great neighbor, she showed me how to put stitches on and then to proceed with the simplest pattern. She used a nice heavy, red wool and said it would look great as a man's scarf. So I was hooked. Whenever I sat down with a few minutes to spare, I would pick up "my knitting". I got along famously. Granted, my scarf wasn't too wide but length made up for it.

After a couple of weeks the article became cumbersome and I wanted to end it but wasn't sure how to do that in case it would unravel. Bea came and cast off the stitches and my work was done. Except for the occasional gap here and there, it was a work of art. Proudly I presented it to my husband and advised it was to be worn with his parka, and I made sure it was included in his supplies when packing for a trip.

Funny, I thought one day, he never mentions his new scarf. Guess he's saving it. Actually I thought it looked smart, adding a touch of color to his navy parka. Granted, it went around his neck several times and there was a rather long tail hanging below the parka. Nothing was said just then. But a couple of weeks later when he returned from patrol in the mountains to a native camp, he handed me the scarf all rolled up in a piece of canvas.

I asked him why he did that and he said, "The damn thing kept tripping me when I bent over to help push the toboggan up the steep hills and the natives asked me if I had a wound in my neck." Then he added "I could have been choked to death and no one would ever suspect it was my wife who had engineered my fate."

Diamond Cee

The main cause of most problems was a native called *Diamond Cee*, a self proclaimed Medicine Man. The natives really feared him because he vowed he could make bad medicine on them, and he encouraged the young men to assert themselves and take matters in their own hands.

On special occasions, the local Band held Tea Dances where they danced (singly) in a circle to the beat of parchment-thin drums. We attended one of these happy gatherings where the rhythm of the drums accompanied by the shaking of bags of mystical herbs and animal parts, created quite an impressive sight. The only drawback was that the cabin was so small and the ventilation so poor that we were nearly overcome by the heavy air of sweat and warm moose-hide. However, the natives really enjoyed it and shed any inhibitions they had even with us watching so close by. Believe me, it was a heartening sight to see them having such a good time.

It was after one of these fêtes that someone reported hearing Diamond Cee bragging about his murder of a young child, having struck the youngster's head a strong blow with a tin cup. The body was placed in a box and hoisted up into the branches of a tree—a tree grave.

Later, Jim and his interpreter Willie MacLeod, were intrigued with the murder story, so they decided to investigate. Willie knew the area where the tree grave was reported to be and before long they had located the little coffin. Carefully, they lowered it to the ground. Inside they found the skeleton of a small child. The hair appeared to have grown quite long but upon close examination they could not detect any sign of violence. Carefully replacing the tiny box back up in the tree, they left. Willie swore Jim to secrecy.

A few weeks later, while Jim was away on patrol, Diamond Cee got roaring drunk on homemade wine and losing control, assaulted his wife. She ran away from him and headed for the Detachment. Upon reaching our back door, she pounded urgently on it and burst into our kitchen. Diamond Cee was gaining on her as she fled into our bedroom and hid behind the dresser. He tried to follow but stopped when I stood in front of the bedroom door, blocking his entry.

"Where do you think you are going?" I asked him.

"I'm going to take my wife home and teach her a lesson," he snarled drunkenly, unsteady on his feet.

I was plenty scared of this drunken, big man but I tried not to show it. I shouted, "Get out—right now!"

He just stood there, glaring at me, not moving. I reached around the bedroom door and pulled open the top dresser drawer. Not taking my eyes off him, I put my hand in and felt Jim's service revolver lying on top of his shirts. I pulled it around and pointed it at his chest. He threw his hands up, "Go ahead, shoot me, shoot me," all the time backing crookedly toward the kitchen door. I slowly walked toward him as he retreated. Luckily for both of us the door was still open and he disappeared into the dark. Right then I slammed the door shut and locked it. I didn't know if the gun was loaded or not, but then, neither did Diamond Cee.

Later he was charged by the Justice of the Peace and received a month in jail for disorderly conduct and assaulting his wife. Being sent to jail was not a harsh sentence. We didn't have a cell and any prisoners we had lived in the office. Fortunately for me, it was a separate building and prisoners were usually only confined at night. Throughout the day, they worked alongside the two men in charge. Although Diamond Cee considered himself the Medicine Man and above manual labour, he did his share and we had a record amount of winter firewood that year. While he was in custody, he received the same meals as we prepared and once he said, "I feel good, missus."

Eventually he tried to teach us some of the Slave language but the vocabulary consists of under one hundred words, one word having several meanings. For instance the word "klea" could mean gas, dog, flour or lard! The context denoted the word to be used. Diamond Cee and his wife brought us a gift of moccasins when our posting was up and we were leaving the settlement, obviously bearing no resentment for his time spent in custody.

Christmas in the Wilderness

This time of year meant a week-long holiday with lots of anticipation for young and old alike. The Christmas mail had arrived by plane two days before, as part of only four regular scheduled deliveries a year. There were several mail bags for us; some were official, the rest personal—lots of cards and presents from relatives 'outside.' Not only the kids were excited!

Well now, with Christmas nearly upon us, the boys kept wondering how Santa Claus could get there without a dog team. Late one evening, one little fellow ventured out of his room, followed by the other.

"Where do you think you're going, young man? Back to bed you go, and take your brother with you."

"But Mom," the four-year-old argued, "we heard Santa Claus. He's coming in the back trail. We heard the bells and you'll make us miss him," he wailed.

"Those were the native families coming to town with their dog teams. We saw four groups making their way down the Hay Lake Trail," I replied. "Now back to bed or you'll scare Santa away. You know he won't come if he knows you're still up."

"Mom," said the younger boy, not yet three, "Do you think he'll remember to bring my gum?"

Good heavens, I had completely forgotten to get the darn gum. As quickly as I could, I pulled on my moccasins and parka and slipped out the back door. It was cold but calm and although it was –50° F., I decided not to bother with ski slacks over my thinner pants. I knew if I ran fast to the Bay, I wouldn't mind the cold, but the inside of my knees stung for several days with frostbite. But gum we had—Juicy Fruit!

Just before the eventful day I was reading a bedtime story to the two lads and the last one I read was 'Twas The Night Before

Christmas. When I came to the part where Santa was leaving to go up the chimney I read: 'and placing his finger aside of his nose'. Well, my older boy, Jamie, grabbed my wrist and exclaimed, "Mom, Mom, how come Santa can blow his nose with his finger when you said if you ever caught Dad doing that you'd brain him?"

Sometimes a parent can't win.

Christmas day dawned clear and cold. We were up early and lit the Coleman lanterns. The kids didn't need a wake-up call as they came racing out of their bedroom into the kitchen still in their Doctor Denton sleepers.

With exclamations of "Look what I got, Dad!" the two little boys turned their Christmas stockings upside down and all their loot escaped onto the floor. Out fell ribbon candies, toy candy and of course, gum! The living room was invaded next. Gaily wrapped presents surrounded a Christmas tree busily decorated with homemade ornaments. My husband and I tried to keep track of all the little "to" and "from" cards in the melee but soon we gave up and joined in the fun.

Now there were several widows who lived in our settlement. Usually two ladies lived together as their respective families had left them to fend for themselves. They shared a tent warmed with a small stove in the center that was lit by candles or coal oil lamps. I had heard that at this time of year, these widow ladies could drop in at any time expecting to receive a Christmas treat. They spoke no English but they smiled a lot. Their visit was a gesture of good will.

Sure enough, one day we found ourselves entertaining five of these women who had simply walked in the door. They made their way through the kitchen to the living room. On our living room floor we had a large polar bear rug. The ladies skirted around this rug and sat down on the floor. As I had been forewarned, I had baked a batch of brownies in anticipation of their visit. To make a favorable impression, I added a few precious walnuts to the brownie mix. I arranged the Christmas treats on a plate and began to pass them around. You can't imagine my consternation when the first lady took the plate and dumped its entire contents onto her skirt in her lap. She then calmly handed the empty plate back to me. I didn't know what to do.

I caught myself staring at her, then realized I still had four remaining guests. I fled to the kitchen and returned with thick slices of our freshly made bread, smothered in strawberry jam. Well, I might as well have saved my precious walnuts because they seemed to appreciate the bread even more than the brownies.

Nature in the North

Mosquitoes

Nature was good to us, but unfortunately, she was also good to the mosquitoes. They multiplied by the second. Whenever you went for a walk, you had to carry a branch to ward them off. Even when the wind was so strong that the birds had to walk, the mosquitoes would take a bite, affecting some inaccessible spot you couldn't scratch in public.

Wolves

Our friend Jack Sime, the Independent Fur Trader, dropped in to return a magazine he had borrowed earlier. As he filled his rather smelly pipe, he looked at my husband and said, "Do you know Jim, I think I'll get rid of my dogs. I just don't have the time to exercise them and it costs a good bit to feed them."

Jim stopped cleaning his rifle and looked up at his friend. "Well," he said, "if you're not getting the work out of them, I guess you'd be justified in selling them. You're kept quite busy, I know, with the store and grading the furs that come in. I heard that Joe Dogrib was looking for a lead dog. Maybe he'd take your whole team."

"I'm glad you mentioned that," said Jack. "He's not too far away and I'll get word to him when the next boat goes down-river."

"You can always borrow my team if you decide to take Peg for a drive some decent day," suggested Jim.

"No way," said Jack as he rose to return home. "I wouldn't dare take the wife out for a run with that team of yours. They're wild when they start out; they go flat out for the first couple of miles and I'd be left behind on my backside. No thanks, the wife would never speak to me again." Then with a twinkle in his eye he said, "That might not be so bad either, only kidding, gotta go," and pulling on his cap, he headed for the door, waved goodbye and left.

Summer passed and the fall chill set in. John Forrest (the Bay Manager) and the RCMP were stocking up on a winter's supply of wood when Jack suddenly realized he had no way of hauling logs to his yard. Of course, he could hire a native, but the ones who were not on a trap line didn't care what kind of wood they used. He could end up with a hollow stump for all they'd care.

Jack inquired about available dogs from various natives and was told of a trapper who had a bitch with four good-sized pups and their mother. He bought them and tied them to individual stakes not far from his back door. The first night the new dogs howled hours on end. The second night was a repetition of the first, but Jack reasoned that they would get accustomed to their new home soon, so merely going out to the back shed, he cracked his whip and they quieted down.

It was a sad sight that Jack was greeted with next morning. All that was left of the forty pound pups was the head of each one, still chained to their stakes. The wolves had dragged off the bodies. Worse still, they had returned the next night and killed the mother. He felt bad not only for his financial loss but for his hope of raising a fine team.

We were wary of wolves reported in or near our settlement. The natives said there was evidence of more than twenty wolves in a pack on trails across the river. In fact, one night our dogs set up a great commotion and looking out our bedroom window we saw a large black wolf skulking along right underneath the window. He was headed back to where our dogs were tied. Our smallest dog 'Toby' was getting frantic and alternately barked and howled.

Jim flew out the back door and fired a shot into the air for he couldn't take a chance of hitting a dog. The noise of the 30-30 rifle scared the wolf and he took off, crashing through the brush out the back trail. Next day Jim set a # 4 trap for him and two days later he was back. This time he got caught and was disposed of. We were relieved because our little boy, Jamie, used to wander out there although he was warned to keep in sight of the dwelling house. After he saw Willie holding the dead wolf, he never went out that way alone again.

Wind

Our Detachment house was situated on a slight rise, about 150 yards from a steep bank, leading down to the fast flowing Liard River. Directly across the river, the hills grew into mountains, and between the high points, a draw existed. Through this gap we could hear the roar of an impending chinook.

One morning, after my year-old son Davie had finished his breakfast, I put him in his "Jolly Jumper" which was a canvas seat suspended from the top of the door frame. Because the seat was held by springs, he could just touch the floor and activate the swing-like toy with his feet. He loved

Willie with the wolf caught just behind our house.

being in it and I had a few minutes peace to finish a chore or two, but was still able to keep an eye on him. As I looked out the kitchen window, I saw a piece of cardboard blowing across the yard. I was surprised as the morning seemed so calm but then I heard the wind roaring through the draw across the river. Glancing out the front room window, I saw the door to the verandah move. I quickly put the pot of hot water back on the stove and as I turned, the kitchen door started to close and the wind drove it with such startling force that I couldn't get to the swing with the youngster in it in time to grab him. However, just at the critical time, Davie's feet touched the floor and he playfully pushed himself back as the door slammed shut, right where he had been sitting. If the little fellow had been going forward, he would have been killed outright. As it was, the door frame was splintered from top to bottom.

I was shaking as I lifted the little boy out of his hanging seat but it didn't faze him one bit as it was so sudden. When I saw the young life spared, I believed the Indian Great Spirit was present even with me. My feeling was that God appears in many ways. In fact, that wasn't a chinook wind. It was just a wayward gust.

76

When the chinooks did arrive, they came with their boisterous roar and the temperature could fluctuate from –50° F. to +50° F. in a very short time. But it could be a busy time! A big copper tub on the top of the stove was quickly filled with snow and then water was dipped from the reservoir attached to the firebox side of the big camp stove. When it was completely melted, we'd wash our Hudson Bay blankets. They seemed to weigh a ton as we carried them out to the clothesline to blow dry. Believe it or not when they were hung out about ten o'clock in the morning, by three in the afternoon they had blown completely dry and were so sweet-smelling. However, if one was traveling by dog team during a chinook, the traveler would have to make camp for the rest of the day as the going would be too hard on the dogs and also time would be needed to firm up the trail again. For every action often there is a reaction and we always experienced ours in the form of a storm next day. But at the time, the chinook wind was a much appreciated respite from the seemingly endless cold.

Bush Pilots

Although we only had four scheduled mail deliveries a year, we got to know the pilots personally as they stayed overnight and we three women 'in town' would invite them to meals. They were welcome visitors.

Sometimes a local run would be made from Fort Nelson to an outlying native camp. This would be done by a young chap whose name was Ray Carruthers. He flew a Piper Cub and was hoping to build up a local flying service.

He had one unfortunate experience while flying to a native camp to deliver some medicine from Fort Nelson. After making his delivery he proceeded to return home by way of Liard in order to drop off another prescription to a native there. The weather had turned colder and the wind had suddenly picked up. Ray decided he'd take a short cut and go cross-country. Suddenly the little plane gave a jolt and began to shudder. Ray knew he had trouble but had no idea what had gone wrong. The plane was starting to vibrate heavily and there he was in the middle of nowhere with no radio, unable to contact the RCAF Search and Rescue at Fort Nelson to report his location. Anxiously he scanned the land below knowing he had to put the plane down quickly or it might crash. Suddenly he saw a clearing and with the vibration increasing, he managed to set the plane down roughly on the solid sandbar of a river.

Ray climbed out and checked the front of the plane and saw that the propeller was damaged. Looking it over more closely, he saw that a nut was missing—it must have come loose and hit the propeller, knocking a sizeable piece off one blade, causing the awful noise and the violent vibration. He looked around and knew he would have to walk out. Luckily for him he had made it as far as the river which he knew from his map to be the Black River, a tributary of the Liard.

He started out, glad there was no snow yet so he would be able to find a trail if there was one along the river. But it was cold, well below freezing. Still, Ray realized the heavy frost had been his ally; it had provided a solid landing surface. He also knew he'd have to hurry as darkness came early this time of year and he didn't know how far he'd have to walk. Picking up his rifle, he set off at a brisk pace.

In the meantime, back at Sime's Trading Post, a native had come in for tobacco and he asked Jack if there was any word of a plane from Fort Nelson. Jack said he hadn't heard anything and asked why. The native told him that a small plane was flying some medicine down to his brother's camp that day and the pilot had said he would stop at the Trader's store and leave some for him also as he had two sick children.

Jack listened to the native and he thought, it's strange. Ray was so reliable and trying to build up his business. He'd never miss a passenger nor a delivery.

Hours went by. Jack became worried. Finally, he came to the Detachment to see Jim and relayed the story told to him by the native. Both men agreed that it didn't sound like Ray so they decided right then to leave on a search.

"I think I'll make a couple of sandwiches for you two just in case 'you' get lost," I said. "So far, I don't think either one of you ever missed a meal in your lives."

"Well, if we don't need them, maybe Ray will," Jim said. "But I'll tell you what I'm going to take and that's 'The Bug'."

Jack looked startled, "What the heck do you mean 'take a bug?"

"It's not 'A' bug, it's 'The Bug', I said. "I'm surprised you haven't patented it by now." And with that remark I went out to the porch and brought in the article.

"Here it is, nothing to it; just a lard pail with a hole in the bottom and up through that hole you insert a long candle. Leave enough of the candle sticking out the bottom for a handle, light the candle inside and away you go.

"Well, won't the wind blow out the candle for Pete's sake?" asked Jack.

"No, the candle is surrounded by all sides. It's great if you have to go outside at night, you can set it down, you don't have to hold it like a flashlight. No batteries and in the dark it really works well."

Jim stuck the sandwiches in the lard pail, picked up his rifle, gave me a hug and followed Jack out the door.

As the two men followed the trail along the Black River for about eight miles, night began to threaten. Little did they know it was also threatening Ray. By this time, he had covered fifteen miles or so and it was getting harder to see.

Jack and Jim stopped at a clearing and stood very still, listening for any sound that might provide a clue. Finally Jim said, "Well, we don't hear any wolves so far but it is early yet and maybe tonight that'll change. Now aren't you glad I took the 'Bug', Jack?"

Poor Jack, never having seen the tin-can lantern being used before, looked skeptical but said nothing. He had seen stranger things happen in this country. Ingenuity was an unpredictable thing.

Jim put shells in his rifle and fired three shots in the air. You could hear the echoes all around as they rebounded off the rocky hills. The silence that followed was deafening.

Then, suddenly off in the distance, they heard one shot, then another. The two searchers looked at each other. "Ray, that's got to be Ray, let's go!" cried Jack and they took off up the trail. There coming around a rocky bend in the trail appeared Ray and with a welcome shout, he approached them.

"Boy, am I glad to see you two old reprobates. You'll never know how good you look to me!" And with that, Ray shook hands with each man in turn.

Don't think the two searchers weren't just as happy. They didn't mention it out loud but around every curve of the trail, they had been afraid they'd come upon a downed plane and an injured (or worse) friend.

Together they returned to the settlement which was in complete darkness by this time. Luckily the path was well worn the closer they got to the Liard and of course, the tin-can lantern was able to prove itself effective.

Dropping Jack off at his home Ray and Jim proceeded to the Hudson's Bay store hoping they'd be in time to put a message on the wireless schedule that evening.

And they made it! Ray sat beside John while he sent a message to Fort Nelson requesting a new prop, giving the details to the mechanic there and two days later it arrived.

Ray presented the original propeller to Jim who thought he'd make it into a clock. Of course, he never did. Just didn't get around to it!

Luck or Skill?

"Listen, is that a plane I hear or an inboard boat coming around the bend of the river?" It wasn't time for a scheduled flight but any visitor was so welcome, sometimes I wondered if we embarrassed them.

Jim straightened up from repairing a slat in the board walk. "Yes, that's a plane alright. Doesn't sound like he's too far away either," replied my husband. The roar of the motor increased as the plane appeared over the trees.

"I wonder where he's headed? He seems to be coming down this way," I said. And in a couple of minutes the bush plane landed with a smack on the water right in front of our place.

"Not such a great landing. I wonder if he had trouble making it this far," mused Jim as he started toward the river where the plane was holding its own against the current. Approaching the float, Jim grabbed the line the pilot threw him and secured it to a nearby post.

"Hi Jim, glad you're home. I wasn't sure if she'd make it here or not. Guess you noticed how the old girl was laboring the last few miles. I think I've got a broken rod or something," and with that Ron Cameron put his hand out to shake hands with Jim and together they turned to climb the bank to the house.

"Where did you come from?" Jim asked.

"Well" replied Cameron, "I left Yellowknife, heading for

Watson Lake but I thought I'd better set her down here on the river. It's a little hard landing in the spruce when you're on pontoons. I will have to take a look and see if it's anything serious. Do you think you could tow it across the river where I can tie up to those big trees? Then I can take a look. I have an idea the cowling is shot."

"No problem," replied Jim, "I'll just get my Special to help; the more the better." He went back to the work shop where Willie was working. Together the three men took our big freighter canoe and towing the plane, they went directly across the river to the far side.

Once the plane was tied up securely, Cam examined the motor. "Look at this!" he exclaimed. "Cowling's shot, broken rod, the engine's finished for this trip at least. I was sure lucky we stayed up long enough to get this far. I can just imagine me sitting on a sandbar up the Nahanni or down on the MacKenzie River. Does the Bay still have a schedule in the evening?" Cameron asked.

"Yup," said Willie. "John has a 'sched' every evening, six o'clock."

"Well," Cam said, "I'll have to contact Yellowknife to send over a new motor. Do you mind if I stay with you for a couple of days—or even a week?"

Oh boy! I thought, I hope he won't mind sleeping in Jim's office. I don't mind the meals but we have only two bedrooms and the boys are there. I hope Cam doesn't mind mice because they share the office too, especially at night when it's quiet.

The men got the wire off that night and two days later a Beaver aircraft arrived with the new engine. The three men, Jim, Willie and Cameron enlisted a fourth chap, Joe Donta, a strong and reliable native, to help.

First they stabilized the floating plane, then tied heavy ropes to the engine, the ends thrown up over the strongest limbs, letting them land on the ground, then tying them to the engine. Their hope was to winch the heavy engine up and then push it on the front. It would take the three men to pull and guide it to the front and the fourth (the pilot) to eyeball the engine when he thought it ready to be pushed on.

One was guiding, two were struggling and the pilot was praying just a little bit.

"Now!" shouted Cameron and the men pushed the motor. They couldn't believe their eyes. The motor fit perfectly. All those bolts went right on the first and only try.

The pilot was speechless—a rare condition for Cameron. He said he had watched trained mechanics wrestle with engines trying to get an exact fit taking many minutes and here it fit the first attempt with the help of two natives and one policeman. He never took any credit for his skill in knowing when to say 'Now'.

Bush pilots were in a distinguished class all by themselves and one well-known and highly respected pilot was John Nesbitt. Raised in the Ottawa Valley he got his license and taught flying for some time then joined the Air Division of the RCMP. Not only was he an excellent pilot, he was a true friend and devoted father, so proud of his son and daughter we sometimes had to change the subject for him. His motto was "Safety First" and he never abused it.

One time he dropped in en route to Dawson Creek and just missed seeing Jim who was out on patrol for several days. John went outside and checked the water barrels. Finding them only one third full, he took the yoke and two pails and made enough trips to the river to fill those two forty-five gallon drums. That was the thoughtful kind of person he was.

Another time, Jim said he and Johnnie were flying up the Nahanni when they were suddenly engulfed by dense clouds. They no longer knew where the mountain peaks were and lost their bearings. Suddenly John saw a tiny opening in the clouds so he just dropped that plane straight down and there below was a perfectly sunny day.

Luck or skill? How about a greater Presence?

So you see, we weren't deprived of the important things in life just because of our isolation. We had a wealth of time-honoured, reliable characters whom we could depend on to teach us some of what was worth knowing, but never enough.

Flight of the Birds, Reindeer

As I glanced across the cozy living room of our northern home, I studied my husband sitting in his favorite chair, a book on his lap, and his feet resting on a homemade foot stool. He looked contented and relaxed after a full day's work. He and Willie had sawed a large pile of logs and his leisure time was well deserved.

"Well," I said, "Jamie is tucked in for the night, time to relax and enjoy the togetherness. This is the best part of the day."

Even if we didn't carry on a running conversation we were content with the presence of each other's company. I thought he's so much like my Dad, quietly efficient, never rough, neither in speech nor action. I wondered if that was another reason why I married him. Was it a father image? Maybe so, maybe not. He filled my life completely.

The silence of the north which filled the room was suddenly broken by the sound of birds, many birds. At first their cries were faint, then gradually louder until you felt their presence overhead.

"What in the world is that noise?" I said, and I got up to go outside to see what was happening. Jim followed me.

It was a clear, cool night with a full moon and the sky above was filled with calling birds. Some flew across the face of the moon making a lacy silhouette. Around and around they flew, always in a large circle and calling out to one another in what seemed frantic excitement. This went on for about fifteen minutes, until suddenly, some mysterious urge caused one of them to veer off and the rest followed flying in a southerly direction. Once more it was quiet and solitude restored.

Next day, Willie told us that he too had witnessed the flight and said they were cranes that had lost their bearings. He said the Great Spirit had heard their cries and directed them back on their migrant path. Nature ever present was once again their guide.

Two days after the flight of the lost cranes, Jim received a visit from a native who lived across the river. He spoke English quite well, having attended a mission school for two years. His name was Alexi and he proudly presented Jim with a parcel wrapped in brown paper. "Here's something for your missus," he said.

Jim brought the gift over to the house. "Take a look at this," Jim stated. "Alexi brought this gift for you," and he handed me the small package.

"What's this?" I asked, "It looks like a catcher's mitt."

"Don't you know what that is? It's a real delicacy and Alexi saved it just for you. It's a moose nose."

I picked up the treasured gift and walked out the back door. The last Jim saw of the nose, it was winging its way over the wood-pile.

Reindeer Round-up

Jim said one of the most interesting things he enjoyed while serving in the Western Arctic was the reindeer round-up on Richardson's Island, located close to the mouth of the MacKenzie River and the Beaufort Sea.

This reindeer herd consisted of approximately 5,000 head, directly under the supervision of a superintendent who resided on a reindeer station approximately 50 miles from the old Aklavik. He was assisted by Eskimo herders and a few reindeer dogs similar to sheep dogs. These reindeer provided a livelihood for the Eskimos: fresh meat, skins for clothing, also hides for footwear.

In the late spring or early summer, the superintendent would visit the herd assisted by the herders, and using a three-foot strip of burlap he would cull out about ten or so reindeer, steer them into a corral where the Eskimo men would then throw each animal and castrate it.

Then, in the late fall, just before freeze-up, the superintendent would return to this herd accompanied by the RCMP, mission and other groups, and assisted by the herders, they would walk amongst the herd picking out the ones that had been castrated in the spring and shooting the required number to supply fresh meat. The herd would be driven back and the carcasses picked up by the various groups, dressed, then placed in a scull for transportation back to Aklavik. Our diesel powered boat was sheathed with iron bark thus allowing us to tow our barge through the young ice. Otherwise, the ice would eventually cut through the soft wood.

Nahanni Tragedy

One fall in mid-November Jim and Willie decided to make a patrol to South Nahanni to check on conditions of the natives in that area. By dog team it was a distance of 85 miles, one way.

The next two days the men repaired and inspected their harness and collected the rations that would be cached along the way to be available if any emergency arose. Sometimes I think they were glad to get away and renew old friendships.

Willie with his dog team

Jim and his dog team en route to Nahanni

They set out on a frosty morning, around –22° F. but the dogs were rested, the trail was firm and they fairly flew the first two or three miles. Then the team settled down to a steady trot and they swung from the bush trail out onto an old route on the river. It was colder without the protection of the spruce, but it was easier on the dogs.

About three-thirty in the afternoon, the men and their two teams left the river trail and stopped at a sheltered clearing where they had made camp on previous trips. There they pitched a tent and while Jim fed the dogs, Willie cut some boughs to put under their sleeping bags. With the heat from their little metal stove they were very comfortable and by the light of a Coleman lantern, they drew a rough map for future reference.

The night faded into a grey and cold dawn. After a hearty breakfast of thawed bannock and beans, they broke camp and set off on the remainder of their trip. In the early afternoon, the men arrived at a trapper's cabin. What a noisy welcome they received from their friend's dogs! The trapper's name was Turner. He not only trapped for a living, but ran a little trading post to accommodate the few native families living along the river. He welcomed the two police and after they had tied up their teams a safe distance from the resident dogs, they went for a welcome cup of tea. Like most Northern travelers, they relished their tea and seldom made coffee on the trail. Turner's cabin was made of logs and their living quarters were very cozy. His wife, Vera, was a real homemaker with several afghans and rugs on the walls and chairs, the bright colors bringing out the gold color of the peeled logs.

The group sat around for quite some time discussing the price of fur and which hides brought in the most money. Then Turner told them he had some disturbing news and that he was glad they had come as he had intended to send a message to ask them for their help.

He told them that the group of natives living near him couldn't travel further up the Nahanni River because the water was too low and their hunting and trapping was too limited where they were in Headless Valley. Dick got to know them as they frequented his store for staples.

This group consisted of about two dozen natives, among them a newly married couple; a man had married a young native girl who had been brought up in the Roman Catholic Mission. He was the brother of a very domineering woman who had elected herself leader and chief of the group. She was very jealous of the younger woman and often ordered the girl to do menial tasks, while forbidding the girl's husband to help her.

After several months of physical and mental abuse, the young wife felt she could stand it no longer and secretly planned to run away one night. Trying to escape without being detected, she didn't dare take down her warmest parka which was hanging above her husband's head, but simply put a deerskin jacket over her sweater, then silently crept out of the tent. She carried her moccasins a short distance, then pulled them on over her damp socks, tying them around the cuffs of her slacks. She knew it was a cold night to run away but her mind was made up, she didn't care that it was well below zero. She was desperate.

Running quietly down the trail that led over a small mountain to South Nahanni, she soon came to a fork in the path and, becoming confused, she followed the one to the right. On she jogged, but slowly realized she had gone in the wrong direction when her path faded out. It had led to a favorite hunting area where it ended.

Discouraged and desperately tired, she thought she'd rest for a few minutes and crept under the sweeping branches of a big spruce. The extreme cold lulled her into a deep sleep and as she drifted off, she told herself she'd continue as soon as she had a rest. Her rest lasted all night, well into morning. In the meantime, the sky had clouded over and the snow fell covering her tracks.

The next day she was reported missing. At first her husband thought she might be visiting a friend who had been teaching her how to fashion beadwork but on checking, realized she wasn't anywhere close by and a search party was formed.

Half a day later, she was found huddled in the snow, under the branches of the big spruce. She told them her feet had no feeling and she couldn't walk. They were frozen.

Taking her back to camp, they feared she would likely lose her feet and worse, she might die. With their belief that when one died their shelter had to be destroyed, she had to be put in a tent away from other members. The young woman was moved to a tent 8 feet by 10 feet, given one blanket but no food, no heat. Her husband was forbidden to give her help of any kind. She had matches and if she wanted to make a small fire at the entrance of the tent she had to crawl on her hands and knees to get wood. Her husband would steal odd scraps of meat and slip them under the tent flap at night.

This was the report given to Jim and Willie by the trapper and his wife. Later that evening, the two men decided to return to Fort Liard in order that they might request the use of the police plane to fly in and rescue her. Next morning, they set off on their return trip home. Their trails were still clear and they wasted no time, although it still took two days.

A wire was sent out on the Hudson Bay wireless and two days later the plane arrived with the pilot prepared to fly direct to Headless Valley. The two men took one team of dogs in case they couldn't land near the camp.

As luck would have it, a native heard the plane coming and stuck small spruce trees in the snow, marking a landing site. Jim, Willie and the pilot were able to walk to the tent where they found the young woman inside. The odour was overpowering. She had been kept there six weeks and when Jim unwrapped the ragged blanket from around her frozen feet, he found her ten toes were black with the bones protruding two inches where flesh had been eaten away by gangrene. She was also pregnant.

Hurriedly, the men made a stretcher and carried her to the plane. The weather was starting to close in, so quickly they took off and flew to the hospital at Fort Simpson, on the MacKenzie River. The resident doctor at Fort Simpson Hospital kept her there until her baby was born at which time she passed away.

Jim had the husband charged with neglect, and he was found guilty, receiving three and a half years in the Prince Albert Penitentiary.

Behind the Roman Catholic cemetery at Fort Simpson, Northwest Territories, stands a little cross marking a small grave. No word was received regarding the fate of the baby, but in all likelihood it would have been adopted into the band and cared for as one of their own.

Davie's Walk

Have you ever experienced fear? I mean the gripping kind that blanks your mind and allows instinct to take over, sometimes irrationally, prompting you to do the worst thing you could possibly do. I experienced that state of panic one warm summer day.

The supply freighter was docked on the Liard River in front of the Detachment and the purser was overseeing the unloading of supplies. It was an activity my two and a half year old son Davie had never seen before and he wanted to go down the path for a closer look. "Let's go, Mum," he coaxed, "let's go see."

The little lad was totally mesmerized by the big slings that raised the large crates in the air, then swung them over to the bank. One of the deck hands asked me if a certain case was destined for the Detachment. I told him I wasn't sure but I'd ask my husband who was signing shipping receipts a few feet away. Getting a negative answer, I turned back to the deck hand and suddenly realized our little boy wasn't standing beside me anymore.

As I looked around, I could feel the panic starting to build. Where was he? Not with his father, no, he had come down to the boat with me. I ran to the back of the freighter, my heart in my mouth and looking up at the outside of the boat, I saw the little tyke just starting to walk on the extremely narrow ledge which ran from the stern to the bow of the boat. Seized with terror, I was about to scream, "Come away from there!" when the purser grabbed my arm and putting his finger to his lips, he shook his head, motioning for me to be quiet. "Don't startle him," he whispered. "That ledge is only six inches wide. He might turn to answer and he'd fall overboard." The river water was swiftly flowing about seven feet below.

How long is a minute? This one seemed a lifetime. I was terrified, watching our little boy slowly putting one foot in front of the other, no railing to hold on to and a solid wall on his other side.

Suddenly he stopped. "Oh Lord," I prayed, "please guide him.

How is he going to turn around? He'd never manage it on that tiny ledge."

The little fellow raised one hand and scratched his neck, and then, as composed as if he were walking across the kitchen floor he continued on, keeping his focus on the bow of the boat. Finally, he reached the broad bow up front and with great confidence, stepped over to where his father was waiting. His Dad grabbed him, hugged him, then lifted him up on his shoulders. He told him he loved him but not when he went on a boat alone. Slowly, the three of us walked up the path to our house. Actually there seemed to be four of us— father, mother, son and the guardian angel.

Preparations For Our Little Girl

"Hello there, can I come in?" Peggy Sime's voice came loud and clear from the back door.

"Of course you can," I called to her. "You're just the person I want to see and to get your opinion on something."

Peg closed the inside back door and pulled off her jacket. "What a nice crisp day for a walk. I just stopped in for a minute at the Bay and thought I'd come along here and see what you're doing." And with that remark, Peg walked into the living room. "For Pete's sake, Jim, what on earth are you doing? I didn't know you could sew. Is there anything you can't do?" She sat down on our chesterfield and watched my husband as he carried on with his work. Peggy had a big smile on her face and if you had been there, you would have understood why.

There sat my mate on the living room floor, one long leg on either side of a portable sewing machine. He was concentrating on a piece of material as he turned the handle to create stitches. Carefully he finished the seam of the article he was working on, then looked up at his friend. "Do you know what I'm doing, Peg? I'm practicing for my retirement; I'm going to hire myself out as a seamster—that's the male version of a seamstress, you know. A person has to look to the future." And with that he turned the material over.

"Say, that's awfully pretty material. Is that the flannelette you sent out for?" asked Peg.

Jim looked a little sheepish and I jumped in to save him, afraid he'd quit. "Yes," I replied, "that's the material I got in the summer mail. Don't you love the little pink rosebuds? And wait until you see the lace I got for the collars of the nighties."

"You're very sure the next one will be a girl, aren't you? I sure hope you're right, but they say the third one changes the pattern. I wish Jack would do things like that for me instead of working in the store all the time. Sometimes I think he goes there to escape," she remarked as she pulled a piece of paper from her pocket. "Here's a wire John Forrest sent over to you, Jim. It just came in on the day's schedule."

Jim took it and opened it. "It's just a circular from Ottawa reporting a missing trapper—nothing specific, just a request to be on the lookout for the chap."He stood up, stretched and made his way outside.

"How many diapers are you making?" Peg asked.

"Oh, I guess about two dozen. You know how long they take to dry, and I'm going to make little flowered pants to go over them. It's a lot more fun preparing for a girl than for a boy, isn't it?" Over a cup of tea we discussed the coming of the October mail plane, both of us hoping a new catalogue would be on it so that we could order things to arrive on the Christmas mail.

Looking at Peggy, I said, "I don't know where I'll be going when the time comes but there's lots of time to decide that. I wish they'd take me to the RCAF hospital at Fort Nelson but you know the rules—no maternity cases, only emergencies."

After Peg left, I started preparing supper. Jim came in with the boys to clean up. "John had a note on the bottom of my communique saying that the Air Force might be down one day soon to make up their required flying hours. Hope they think to bring some fresh fruit for the kids."

Time went by and a week later we heard a plane circle, then land in front of the Detachment on the river. Up the bank came the pilot and mechanic, and accompanying them was a third chap. He was carrying a bag and Jim, on answering the front door, welcomed the flying doctor, Doctor Vic Shearer. He was down with the crew while they completed their required flying hours.

"Come in, come in," Jim urged and soon was enquiring about activities at Fort Nelson and vicinity. The visitors asked the kids what they were busy doing but they were too shy to talk very much. Then the pilot brought out the large bag they had carried to the house.

They gave Jamie an orange and tossed one to Davie, but he didn't remember ever having seen one before and threw it to his brother.

"Here, here," Jim said as he had just returned to the room. "That's no way to handle fresh fruit."

Chastised, the little fellow dropped his head and said, "It's no good, Dad. It's got a cover on it."

The mechanic laughingly peeled the orange, broke it in sections and handed it, one piece at a time, to the youngster who examined it carefully before putting it in his mouth. Then he ate the whole thing.

While this was going on Jim had been talking to Dr. Shearer in the kitchen telling him of our pending arrival, supposedly in February. The good doctor said not to worry, that they'd take care of me and fly me to Fort Nelson sometime around the middle of February. This was a relief to Jim for he had patrols to make and couldn't leave the children alone.

The Long Lonely Wait

With Christmas over, we settled down to answering mail and getting thank you letters ready for the next one. January seems a long month, regardless of where you are. Jim had a couple of long patrols to make before I would go to Fort Nelson to await the arrival of our next addition to the family.

Every day I'd make and freeze different items of food. With the big oven of my kitchen 'camp' stove I mixed up several batches of bread. It accommodated eighteen loaves at a time but it had no heat indicator to give the temperature. I had to determine the heat by the type of wood I burned. To open the oven door I had to pull a steel knob attached to a spring and that would allow the heavy door to be lowered down. After cooling the bread, I'd wrap it and freeze it.

For Jim I'd made big crocks of baked beans, freeze them on a steel sheet, then break them into pieces and store them in burlap bags. When he wanted to use them, he'd put them in a frying pan, add a little snow then place them over a camp fire or the little tin stove in the tent; same with the bannock. Bannock was made like a biscuit dough but cooked in one large sheet, like a cake. I'd cook it, bag it and, sometimes as a treat I'd put raisins in it and call it dessert. Occasionally the natives would give them fish and of course, they gladly swapped canned food for fresh fish any day.

February 2 came—Ground Hog Day—my birthday and mentally I began preparing for my trip to Fort Nelson. About the tenth of the month we received a wire saying the RCAF would be down on the first fine day. I hated the thought of leaving Jim and the boys but had no choice so I was in readiness when they arrived, and said a tearful goodbye to a solemn husband and two little woe-be-gone kids. Jim would be mother and father until I came back.

Staying at Fort Nelson awaiting the pending event had its good points as well as lots of sad lonely hours. I had a room all to myself at the hospital with a window which looked out onto the river and in the moonlight, it looked like a ribbon of steel. At the end of that ribbon was my home, my husband and two little ones. I was very lonesome and the hot water pipes kept banging, especially at night.

Some of the folks on base were awfully kind, especially Betty and Doctor Shearer. They had the dearest little girl whose name was Heather. She looked like a big doll. I couldn't help hoping my little girl would look just like her.

Time dragged on. February turned into March. Our calculations were influenced by hopes. Finally on March 16, time stepped in and with a shot of morphine I climbed on board an RCAF transport plane flying to Edmonton because there were no facilities for maternity cases at Fort Nelson. I was scheduled to go to the University Hospital in Edmonton to await the arrival of our (hoped for) baby girl. I couldn't help but smile to myself while thinking if those chaps sitting opposite me only knew how close I was to term. Landing at Edmonton, I was picked up by an RCMP car and driver and proceeded to the home of Assistant Commissioner Belcher and Mrs. Belcher, who were friends from Ottawa. Mrs. Belcher had made a stew before I arrived but I had to excuse my lack of appetite and left for the University Hospital in the early evening.

It was not long after midnight on March 17 that my "little girl" arrived—great, except it was another little boy. Someone had sent a wire to my folks in Nova Scotia and I received a wire from my parents congratulating me on 'Baby Pat' so I thought that was a logical name but since Jim didn't even know where I was, I couldn't get his opinion of my selection. I decided since we were Scottish that I'd call him Patrick Alexander and if Jim didn't like the name 'Patrick', we could call him Sandy, short for Alexander.

Patrick - 4 months old

On the third day I went home to the Belcher's place and stayed overnight. In the morning, I took the baby down to show Mr. Belcher. He took one look at him and said, "He's a homely little bugger, isn't he?" Still, since the Belchers' didn't have any children of their own, they were very impressed with Patrick's behavior, no crying or fuss and it wasn't long till Mrs. Belcher wrote to say they had adopted a boy of their own.

The next day a neighbor, Mrs. Darling, sent over a beautifully decorated clothes basket for me to take Patrick home. Off we went to the Air Force base where we boarded a plane loaded with large, long pipes lying on the floor of the noisy plane. Patrick was tucked in between the pipes for stability and we flew to Fort Nelson. The plane continued on to Norman Wells with its cargo. At Fort Nelson, I transferred to a Piper Cub and flew within four miles of home, landing on the Black River. Jim met me with the dog team and snuggled down in a nice warm eiderdown. I arrived back home.

Neither of the boys would greet me as they hardly recognized me but my husband was overjoyed to see his new son and to get his housekeeper back.

Patrick

Our latest addition, Patrick, was fitting in nicely with his two brothers, even when he wore his rosebud nightie and flowered matching panties over his diaper. However, I got a big surprise when 'Paddy' was about eight months old. I lifted him out of his morning bath and placed him on a fluffy towel on the kitchen table which overlooked the backyard. As I dried him off, I towelled his golden hair, and to my amazement, it sprang into a mass of yellow curls. I opened the window and fairly shouted to Jim who was in front of his office. "Come quick, come here and see this!" Thinking the worst, Jim ran for the house right into the kitchen.

"What's wrong? What happened?" he said breathlessly.

"Look," I said, "he's got curly hair". "Isn't that something?"

Jim, still visibly shaken but relieved, looked sideways at me and retorted, "You tell him that in 50 years time—if he still has hair then."

What a way to deflate a person but I had the last laugh a few days later when Alexi asked Jim if he could bring his wife, also native, to see the new baby as she had never seen a white baby boy.

"Yes, of course," Jim replied. "Would this afternoon suit you?" Alexi, pleased, went back to get his wife. I scrubbed the little guy and dressed him in his colorful nightie just before Alexi and his wife walked in.

Alexi's wife just stopped and stared at the little fellow. With her hands clasped in front of her she said, very softly, "Oh doya, doya," which can mean several things but since she was smiling, I gathered that it was good. Then she spoke in Slavey and I looked at Alexi as I didn't understand.

He said, "Oh! He looks just like the baby Jesus at Christmas time. She thinks he's an angel."

There was my family, two little devils and one new angel, all equally precious.

Northern Designs

How in the world can I make a parka for my two-year-old son without a pattern? I wondered if our interpreter Willie could find out what the native women used when they sewed. They certainly produced some lovely winter clothes.

"Willie," I said, "what patterns do the natives use when they make parkas?"

He replied, "They don't use patterns. They make the first parka, then copy it for the others."

"Yes, I know that but how do they get started on the very first one?"

Willie said, "Oh that. Well, they take a piece of string and hold it up to the back of the neck, then let it drop down to where the parka should end, then at that length they make a knot in the string. Using the same string they put it around the waist and they make another knot. For the sleeves, they measure from the top of the arm to the cuff—another knot—no need for patterns. All that's needed is a piece of string. He was so serious I believed him and when I asked a native lady to make a parka for Jim, I understood what he was talking about.

The native lady, Mrs. Thomas, came to Jim's office and took Jim's measurements. She kept saying 'Duya, Duya' which could mean lovely, awful or big. It was the adverb 'very' Willie said; she meant 'duya, big' and when she attempted to put the string around Jim's waist, she started to giggle. I could see Jim was getting a little leery about all this measurement stuff but he kept quiet until she was finished. When he asked her if she had enough knots, she just laughed.

The parka, made of light weight canvas, was ready in two days. It wasn't fancy as it was made to be worn as a windbreaker while traveling in the bush—but it was a perfect fit. Around the hood was a strip of wolverine fur, cut on the bias so that it would conform to the head. They always used wolverine because it wouldn't frost up as much as other fur but it was hard to get. If a trapper was unlucky enough to catch a wolverine in his trap, the animal would make a mess of it and everything around it. They were very vicious and very strong. One Native said he saw one throw the hindquarter of a moose over its back and make off with it. What they couldn't eat, they'd urinate on it to spoil it for anything else.

The native women did beautiful silk and quill work. They'd flatten the quills with their teeth and made intricate patterns for moccasins, parkas, whatever they wanted. They also fashioned water containers out of birch bark. They could boil water in them as they were very durable. They called them 'rogans'.

From the trading store the native women picked out the brightest colored duffel cloth to make liners for their mukluks or moccasins and fine cloth for parkas and trim. Thread was a brightly coloured luxury since they usually sewed with babiche. The women did most of the heavy work, including the making of the babiche. They took sinew from the back of a moose, a strip that ran from the neck to the rump. Stretching it between two trees until it dried made it possible to cut it in very fine strips, almost as fine as thread but very strong. This unique material was used to sew their footwear together and the coarser strips were used as snowshoe lacing and webbing.

I watched them make moccasins out of moose-hide and learned how to make my youngster's footwear. It was interesting to see how they used a third narrow strip of moose hide to strengthen

Jamie and David wearing the first mukluks that Betty made

the vamp on the top of the moccasin. But getting all those tucks in the hide required very strong jaws to crimp it and also a goodly supply of patience. Both were in short supply at our house but when the native women saw my finished product, they were very kind and tried to hide their smiles.

Patrick with handmade parka, mitts and mukluks

Our Visitor

One evening just after supper, John Forrest, the Bay manager brought a message over that he had received on his daily wireless schedule. It was the RCMP in Ottawa informing my husband that a reporter and cameraman would be dropping into the Detachment on their way through to Headless Valley. There they planned to collect material to do a documentary on the infamous area. Headquarters requested that Jim assist the men if they had any problems. These two men were employed by the *Vancouver Sun* newspaper. The photographer's name was Art Jones and the reporter's name was Pierre Berton.

It was quite a few days later that the crew arrived. They had been held up at Fort Nelson with plane trouble. The plane itself was quite a relic. It was an old Junker made of metal and the wings gave the illusion of flapping when landing. Also, it was very noisy, metal on metal, different from the nimble and quiet Otter and Beaver aircraft but even worse than the Norseman, classified as 'the work horse of the North.' Anyway, when it landed, Jim went down to greet them and to offer his assistance.

Berton and Jones introduced themselves and asked if their gear could be delivered up the bank to the settlement. Jim told them his team would be brought down and the equipment taken to wherever they were staying. Apparently the *Sun* had made previous arrangements for the reporter and photographer to stay at a Bay post whenever possible. No mention of the pilot or mechanic. They were flying on their own.

After dropping off the heavy equipment at the Bay, Jim felt obligated to invite the pilot and mechanic to stay at our place. We were glad they accepted as they were great company and entertained us with lots of stories of their problems all along their trip.

Pierre Berton later visited us and asked a lot of questions. He wanted Jim to accompany them as a guide into the Nahanni country and point out the main points of interest, such as the Hot Springs, Virginia Falls and Headless Valley.

Virginia Falls on the Nahanni River

When Jim was asked to accompany them, he countered with his one request. Would they consider taking along an Indian woman who had a broken leg? It would mean flying over their proposed destination, dropping the injured woman off at the Fort Simpson hospital, then back tracking to the Nahanni country. This was agreed upon and would likely be publicized as a mercy flight.

Jim Reid just before going with Pierre Berton up the Nahanni

Next morning, the injured native was brought to the plane where she and her youngster were made comfortable. Obviously they were quite nervous, but never said a word. After all, this was their first flight and it was to a hospital.

The plane, with its crew and passengers, set off and, as they followed the Liard River they could see on the left in the distance, the peaks of the Rocky Mountains which soon would be over shadowed by the MacKenzie Mountains, said to be the largest single mountain range in Canada.

On arriving at Fort Simpson, they unloaded their patient and her child on the river bank. They would be taken care of by the Department of Transport and delivered to the hospital which was about twelve or more miles distant.

Then they took off to fly back up the Liard River reaching the mouth of the Nahanni River as it was becoming dusk. In the north, twilight comes early in winter. Baker spotted a cabin at the mouth of the South Nahanni River and set the Junker down on solid river ice.

Jim, the two newspaper men, mechanic and pilot all made their way to the traders's cabin. This man had lived there with his Indian wife for thirty years and he was delighted to have company.

He ridiculed the wild stories that circulated among the natives saying they were figments of the imagination. When the subject of the Hot Springs came up, he said they were about forty miles upriver where Gus Kraus lived and ran a trap line. Some natives said the area was a tropical paradise but that stretched the truth a lot, he felt. Sure, the springs were hot and they were sulphur too. The temperature ranged between 80–89° F. but the snow was deep within fifteen feet of the springs. He was wound up and talked until late in the night. The crew, who already had a full day, were ready for bed. Taking their sleeping bags, they laid them out on the floor in a small front room and finally got some sleep.

Early in the morning they took off, having been warned repeatedly by the trader to watch for rotten ice. It seems no one had ever landed a plane on the Nahanni in winter. This would be the first attempt. Looking over the river as they flew along, they could see channels veering off in different directions. Soon, they saw a wall of rock and ahead of it a canyon which the river had cut out of the limestone. Flying on another fifteen miles or so, they rounded a bend and there below was Deadman's Valley. What a beauty! All of a sudden the pilot shot the plane skyward. He had been about to land when he saw running water. Now he needed to make a couple of runs to get an idea where it would be safe and flat enough to land. Finally, he saw a level area and decided to try to put the plane down on the ice.

The first attempt shook everyone up as the big plane hit the ice and bounced up in the air. A second attempt was also unsuccessful while on the third attempt at landing, they nearly crashed into a six-foot hummock of snow and ice. The plane shuddered but the skilled pilot managed to bring it safely to a halt.

Looking across the frozen river, they saw two old dilapidated cabins. The two newspaper men, Jones and Berton, had been given a sign from the *Vancouver Sun* to tack up while in Deadman's Valley. It would prove that they had made it there. They asked Jim to stand beside it, but since he was in uniform, he declined, imagining Ottawa's reaction. The sign read, "KILROY WAS HERE."

Suddenly, the wind came howling down the canyon. Baker, alarmed by the increasing wail of the wind, told them to get quickly on board the plane and prepare to leave. Actually, they weren't that far from the spot where the MacLeod brothers had been murdered. The story was that while prospecting for gold they had been killed while sleeping in their bedrolls. One story circulated that they had been beheaded, thus originating the name 'Headless Valley.' Willie later revealed to us that the two slain men were his uncles.

Off the plane went, flying over Nahanni's vast area. Below they saw the second canyon at the far end of the valley and then they flew over Hell's Gate. Passing over the Flat River, they came upon the awe-inspiring Virginia Falls and its rushing torrents, reportedly twice as high as Niagara Falls.

Leaving that area, the crew decided to return to Liard, arriving there in the late afternoon. I had prepared a moose dinner and the men cleaned up the stew. The next day after breakfast as they were preparing to leave, Art Jones took several pictures of us with our dog team before Jim hauled their equipment to the plane. Before we said farewell to the adventurers, I presented Russ Baker with a pair of silver fox mitts which I had made. He was pleasantly surprised and thanked me for the gift. He had put up with a lot and I felt he deserved them.

The big Junkers lumbered along the Liard River like a wounded swan, then climbed slowly into the sky and headed west to the Yukon. To give you some idea how cold it was, poor Art Jones' bottle of rum had frozen and burst. The temperature was recorded at –82° F. at Snag.

We later heard that the many pictures taken during the expedition were lost or stolen in transit back to the *Vancouver Sun*. Jim was later mentioned in Berton's book, *The Mysterious North*.

The Greenhorn and Other Characters

"You know, you shouldn't be too critical of a greenhorn. After all everyone has to learn sometime."

These were my very own words as I sat at the kitchen table drinking coffee with two old trappers who were good friends of my husband. I had a lot of respect for them too. By the time I finished the word 'sometime', Andy had dropped his spoon and as it landed on the floor, he left it there and sailed into me with this reminder:

"Hey, what about that new Game Warden just out from the prairies. Now there was a good example of a mess a fellow could get into just because he thought he knew better. He wouldn't listen to any advice. Remember what happened to him. He nearly cashed in."

Well, I did remember. This chap's name was Vic, a rancher straight from the farm. He had landed a job as a game warden and with his new position he was the proud recipient of a large scow, complete with heavy-duty motors, new camping gear and a high-powered rifle. Eager to show his brother his new equipment, he left Fort Simpson and arrived in his new scow at his brother's home which was next door to us.

That evening, all the men came to our place to get acquainted and on leaving, Vic said they were going next door to play cards—probably all night. They had a lot of catching up to do. Vic assured them it wouldn't bother him to lose a little sleep.

"I'll just curl up in the bedroll and let the scow drift with the current down-river to Simpson", a distance of 200 miles.

Both Jim and Jack Sime tried to warn him that the river was treacherous, with several small rapids and fallen logs buried just below the surface.

Vic looked like a small boy who had been unjustly chastised and said, "Don't worry boys, I know what to do. It's no problem."

And with that he left to spend the night playing poker next door.

Very early next morning, Vic took off before we were up. We wondered if he would send a wire back to his brother to let him know he had arrived home safely. No word came.

"Oh well," said his brother. "No news is good news."

About nine thirty that evening, still broad daylight, into our back porch staggered the traveler and what a sight he was! Sun-burned, fly-bitten, clothes badly torn in places and his face swollen so badly his eyes were nearly shut.

"What the heck happened to you!" exclaimed Jim as Vic collapsed on the closest chair.

"I'm exhausted," groaned Vic. "I walked all the way through the bush from across those rapids near Willie's winter cache."

"That's at least twenty miles, maybe more!" exclaimed Jim. "And with no trail. What about the scow and all your gear?"

"Well, I guess I should have listened to you guys," said Vic, "but I was tired after playing cards all night, so when I left this morning I curled up in my bedroll and went to sleep. I would have been alright but that darn scow got caught up in a big deadhead, ran up on one side of it, then tipped over and sank. Everything went down with it. I can't swim but I was lucky. I caught a floating log, wrapped my arms around it and by kicking my feet, I finally got to shore."

Feebly, he continued, "From there I walked along the edge of the river through the dense bush. With no trail, believe me, it was rough going. I was soaking wet, my clothes were torn by sharp branches and the flies nearly drove me crazy. I really thought I wouldn't make it back but I'm sure glad to be here. Guess you fellows knew what you were talking about, but I'll have some tall explaining to do to the Department when I get back, losing all their expensive equipment."

That was a humble admission of one greenhorn. It could have been a tragedy but this time anyway, he was spared.

Ju-sit-see

As time passed, we encountered some unusual characters. One chap, whose name was Ju-sit-see, closely resembled the 'missing link'. He would sit on a nail keg at the Independent Fur Trader's and crack frozen brazil nuts with his teeth. He wasn't what you would call handsome and didn't speak English but he was never out of sorts. The other natives often depended on Ju-sit-see to help them out.

Andy Jensen

Another fellow, a big Swedish trapper and excellent cook, lived in the settlement or fort as it was called. He worked on the Northern Transportation supply boats in the summer as the company cook. His name was Andy Jensen and he was always well groomed and, being of fair complexion and hair, he seemed to shine. He was an avid cribbage player and a great admirer of good rum.

Betty Reid with Andy Jensen

On one trip down North on a supply boat, he had a little too much of a good thing and became sick. Thought he was going to die; in fact he looked forward to it. He lost his dentures in a pail but fished them out, washed them off and set them down on the open oven door of the big oil stove. When his alarm clock went off early next morning, Andy the cook crawled out of his bunk, pulled on his trousers and headed for the galley. Still half asleep, he lit the stove and kicked the oven door shut. It wasn't long before the smell of coffee permeated the morning air and Andy came to life.

Suddenly he remembered his false teeth. Quickly he pulled open the oven door and there they were. However, they had changed quite drastically. Warped and misshapen, some teeth pointed up and some faced outwards. Andy was devastated! There he was en route to Aklavik with lots of people to visit along the way and he had no teeth. Worse still, it would be at least three weeks before he'd be back to where he could catch a plane to Edmonton and find a dentist.

At one of the forts along the MacKenzie River where they had stopped to unload freight, Andy managed to locate some beaver teeth and using glue, he tried to construct a temporary plate. But he had no success, just inconvenience during the trip and no lack of ribbing from the crew.

Another episode with his dear old friend rum was not quite so disastrous. It was New Year's Eve and all the neighbors (two families, two trappers, Jim and I) were at our place to usher in the New Year. We gathered around a big table and played Rummoli. As it neared midnight, all glasses were filled except, of course, Andy's glass was half full. He liked to drink it neat. Suddenly, for no obvious reason, although the table must have been bumped, Andy's glass fell off the table and landed upright on the linoleum floor. Not a drop was spilled. We all looked at Andy. No one said a word but I'm sure we all thought, here's a man with great connections.

Gus and Mary Kraus

"You'll never guess who just docked in front of our place!" That was the statement Jim challenged me with as he walked in the front door. "Look who's here!"

In walked our old friend, Gus Kraus and his wife Mary, a native woman. They had finally made a trip to Liard, coming by powered canoe from Nahanni Hot Springs. With a big smile, he proudly introduced Mary to me. Of course, Jim had already met her several times as he always dropped in on them when in that area.

'The Hot Springs' would dominate the conversation when trappers and adventurous travelers got together in the Nahanni region. Gus and Mary had a big log cabin at the 'Springs', which was sulphur and at a constant year-round temperature between 80–90° Fahrenheit. They were located approximately 40 miles up the Nahanni River but to reach them, one had to be careful of sandbars.

Gus was a prospector and trapper. Mary was the hunter and she never failed to get a moose if she needed one. She tanned the hide, then cut the narrow strips needed to lace the snowshoes after Gus had steamed and shaped the wood. Her footwear, mukluks and moccasins were outstanding: lots of silk work, some quill work also. She was a quiet lady but so interesting when telling us of Gus' latest attempt to grow a new crop. He had a wonderful garden which supplied them with vegetables all year round. He stored them in a cold root cellar dug out of a bank, then cribbed with logs. And what a story teller he was! With hand gestures to emphasize points of his stories, he would have been a star had he performed in public. The best part of it was, he didn't realize how vivid and entertaining his stories were. He was a natural and a real gentleman. They didn't have any children but later adopted a boy named Mickey. Several notable people visited Gus, one of the more famous being the late Pierre Elliott Trudeau. I bet they had fun swapping yarns.

Gus Kraus going up the Nahanni River (First Canyon)

Old John's Coffin

We were told a story about a fellow named "Old John." He lived near the river bank and when he died, he was buried closer to the river's edge. Some said his coffin was visible and really should be moved back. However, the spring before we left, the river rose very high and John and his cabin both went out with the ice.

Bill King

Bill King was another resident in our little settlement. A bachelor, he was a revenuer from England, harmless enough and fairly-well educated. But he had one flaw: he was totally allergic to work. He liked to visit and dropped in daily looking for a cup of tea while he smoked incessantly, rolling his own cigarettes.

Widows O'Shaughnessy and Lepee

Occasionally, Bill King would call on the widowed natives who lived in the woods near the Detachment. They were jolly ladies who didn't understand or speak English but they were very friendly. Living in a tent with only a little metal camp stove for heat demonstrated how self-reliant they were. They chopped their own wood and dragged it to their tent, made bannock on top of their stove, and melted snow for drinking water. They were very fond of my husband Jim as occasionally he would take the dog team and haul a load of dry wood to their tent. How they would chatter and beam—so appreciative for such a small gesture.

Betty Reid with Widows O'Shaughnessey and Lepee

But these two old ladies — widow O'Shaughnessy and widow Lepee—had a disconcerting habit of reaching through their layers of sweaters and picking out annoying, biting, tiny creatures and cracking them with their front teeth. And your presence didn't deter them from this practice. Every month they appeared at Jim's office for ration vouchers that they could take to either the Hudson's Bay store or the Independent Fur Trader's. There they received ten pounds of flour, eight pounds of sugar, five pounds of tea, maybe five pounds of lard and if a new tent was necessary, they received a voucher for that too.

Living in a tent with such a small source of heat was no trial to them, even when the temperature went down to $-74°$ Fahrenheit. But during a severe cold snap one of them stayed up half the night to make sure the fire didn't go out. In the summer when the temperature was slightly more than $90°$ above they threw a blanket over the top of the tent, helping shut out the burning rays of the summer sun and making their small living space cooler inside.

Paul Joe Propochuk

Through our interpreter and Special Constable Willie MacLeod these natives would often inquire about the health of Jim's boss. The first time this happened he was surprised—and puzzled. Where had they heard about his Commanding Officer? Then it was explained to him that the Indians all considered the white man's boss to be the Queen, across 'big water.'

One May after the ice went out, Jim was informed of several break-ins of caches along the river. Upon investigating, he found the culprit, arrested him, and brought him to his office where he was housed until the Justice of the Peace could sentence him.

While he was in custody, he told us he was an artist, that he could paint everything and anything, even Jesus Christ flying. We realized he meant angels. To prove it, he said if we gave him a brush and some paint, he would show us. He said his name was Paul Joe Propochuk.

Well, the only brush we had was a shaving brush. The chap cut it down to a point with a razor blade, then taking some black paint left over from painting the canoe, in no time at all he had created a beautiful scene of a lake with snow-capped mountains in the background. The snow was white paint left over from the house. The golden sun reflecting off the mountain peaks was yellow used in painting the numbers on the canoe and in the foreground spruce trees
112

were effected by black canoe paint. All this was done in less than fifteen minutes on an old piece of wood with the T. Eaton Co. sticker on the back.

When he left our place, he went back up the Alaskan Highway where he made a living painting portraits of American tourists.

A true character.

Brother Halter

In our settlement, the Roman Catholic Mission that Father Levesque was visiting stood on a solitary hill overlooking the Liard River. It commanded a view of the natives encamped directly across the river. It was a two storey building and Father Mary, the priest in charge, knew pretty well everything that went on in his parish.

Living with Father Mary was a helper by the name of Brother Halter. He took care of the menial tasks, constantly supplying firewood and caring for a very large and very bountiful garden. Brother Halter was from Alsace Lorraine. A full grey beard hung down to his stomach, and it bobbed up and down when he spoke. Combined with his broken English, it made him very difficult to understand. He was quite short and appeared to be half human and half whiskers. But he was a man of stature when it came to knowledge.

Although the growing season was short, daylight was almost continuous. His garden was a veritable showplace. He was proud of his crops of cabbage, several of which weighed more than fourteen pounds. Each fall he presented us with a three-pound lard pail full of homemade sauerkraut. Those who liked the stuff said it was excellent.

Brother Halter sometimes dropped in to visit us on a summery Sunday afternoon. He would arrive at the front door, give it a gentle tap and walk in. Invariably, he wore a black homburg hat, a woollen shirt and a heavy black suit coat on top. Woollen trousers—better worn on sub zero wintry days—were tucked into ankle moccasins. And our summers were **hot,** often more than 90° F.

He'd sit upright on a straight-backed chair and his eyes would twinkle as he asked how our garden was growing and also if the children were well. Jim knew he was anxiously waiting for a cigar or a cigarette, always expressing great surprise and profuse thanks when they were offered. Then the suspense began. Brother Halter would strike the match and hold it up to the cigarette. We watched transfixed as he carefully guided it through the maze of beard. However, the most stressful period was when the cigarette burned down to a stub and was barely visible. More than once we heard a little sizzle as a whisker was singed off.

The kind old man also relished his cup of tea and homemade cookies, limiting himself to three or four. As he would leave, I'd slip him a bag with extra cookies in it - I imagine they disappeared before he got back to the Church. In the winter, Brother Halter stayed close to the Mission, while Father Mary traveled by dog team to visit the parish.

The Father was a forbidding, austere man who seldom smiled. He got along well with the men in the settlement but seemed condescending to the women. One winter day, on hearing dogs barking and a bit of shouting, we looked out front to see the Father's dog team racing along the trail at full speed - with the hapless priest dragging along on his stomach. Dressed in his long black robe and still wearing his black triangular hat, he gamely held onto the rope dragging from the front of the toboggan until they all disappeared through a patch of prickly raspberry canes. Still, when we saw him a few days later, he was no worse for wear, or tear.

Apple Cider

One day in mid summer, a boat loaded with freight for the Bay store docked out in front, and the deck hands unloaded several barrels marked, 'Sweet Apple Cider'.

The manager, John Forrest wasn't expecting the shipment so he left it on the main floor of the store where it remained undisturbed for several days. One morning a native dropped in for some fishing line and not being in a hurry, he wandered over to the barrels and looked them over. He asked John what they contained and John told him they were full of apple juice. The chap thought juice came only in cans but he decided he'd try some. John filled a jug and gave it to him to try and the man left.

Next morning before the store was open, the natives were lined up at the door carrying kettles, pots, juice cans—anything that held water. John was happy to sell the stuff and make room for other merchandise. However, unknown to the conservative Scotsman the sweet cider had started to ferment and the natives discovered a ready-made potent drink. It was the best apple juice they had ever drunk.

When John heard what was happening, he was devastated. He could see himself being fired for bootlegging and so he made a bee-line for the Detachment and told Jim of his predicament. Jim had never seen John so upset and I think he had to smile to himself to see the manager, who didn't have a dishonest bone in his body, really in panic over his dilemma. Jim told him to get rid of the stuff as soon as possible. Dump it. Luckily, Carl Arhus was going to Fort Nelson so John asked him to take the cider barrels and dump them on the way. With the scow loaded, Carl started upriver, then remembered that his wife had asked him to pick up a parcel for her from Peggy Sime so he pulled in and tied up.

Peggy had been watching for him and went down to the boat with the parcel. Sitting on a box, she talked to her old friend about gossip along the river and after running out of topics, she got up to go.

As she did so, Carl said, "Tell me Peg, is this sweet or hard cider?" She had never tasted cider before and accepted a long, cool glass of it. Carl told her he had been asked to dump it out.

"Well, that's a very refreshing drink, Carl. I certainly wouldn't get rid of that stuff. Maybe you can use it yourself." And then she accepted another tumbler full. Thanking Carl she left the boat and climbed unsteadily up the bank to her house. After checking on her little girl who was having her afternoon nap, she went straight to her couch, collapsed and fell fast asleep.

It wasn't too long before her youngster awakened and seeing her mother sleeping so soundly she decided to help herself to some homemade bread on the table. She pulled out the silverware drawer but it came out too far, and with a crash it fell to the floor, cutlery scattered everywhere. Peggy never turned a hair until some time later when she woke with a terrible headache. Surveying the mess, she thought she'd never be able to bend over and pick up the scattered silverware.

Later, discussing her experiment with cider, hard or sweet she swore she would never touch that lethal stuff again.

John Shaback

John Shaback pushed his old army cap back on his head. A slight man, about five feet nine inches, with sandy hair and no distinguishing characteristics, he commanded no unusual attention. He was of Russian descent and had just been discharged from the Canadian army, going nowhere in particular. As he ambled along the busy Edmonton street, enjoying a leisurely walk instead of a route march, he wondered what his wife would be doing just then. Likely at work, he thought. She was the cashier at a local dry-cleaning establishment.

His thoughts about his wife were uninspired, almost routine. After eighteen years of married life, a creeping sense of boredom was becoming more evident. Probably it was mutual. As he glanced across the city street, he realized he was near the bar where several of his army buddies usually dropped in for a beer. Looking both ways until traffic cleared, he quickened his steps. Maybe they would have some news of pending jobs or activities available for returned army personnel.

On entering the pub, he saw that most of the individual tables were occupied, with the exception of one off in a corner. He walked over to it and sat down with his back to a group of men. He ordered a beer and when it came, he settled back to relax and enjoy it. The men behind him were discussing their plans and future projects. They seemed to have a strong sense of where they were going and what they intended to do.

One man, who had a slight accent and spoke louder than the others, described his very successful winter the year before. When pressed for details, he said he had a very good trap line in the Yukon where he was successful in harvesting more than one hundred marten and as many mink. His income from the five months work was well up in the thousands. He minimized the amount of effort and risk in the description of his lucrative career. There was no mention of

116

the isolation or discomfort from the extreme cold and nagging lone-liness—just the monetary reward and the good life he enjoyed when he returned to civilization in the spring.

Shaback was fascinated by the man's account of his success. Turning in his chair, he asked where all this good fortune was to be found. The man looked at John and told him that he flew into the Yukon each fall. After he had made a couple of trips, he finally settled beside a lake where he built a cabin and spent the winter establishing a trap line. His description was sketchy at best but Shaback imagined that it would be easy to find, thinking that the Yukon wasn't such a huge area. After all, he just had to find a large lake and maybe a cabin wouldn't be that far away.

Presently, the men at the table behind him got up and left, leaving one inspired listener who felt he finally had gotten a lucky break. By golly, he too would go North and make his fortune. Maybe then Stella, his wife, would have more respect for him and life would be easier.

All this happened early in September, 1947; John Shaback decided he should make plans and arrangements before freeze-up. After inquiring around Edmonton if there was a charter service with planes heading North, he was directed to a company which agreed to supply him with a plane and pilot to fly him out in the middle of September.

In the meantime, his wife had gone to visit relatives in Oregon. John hadn't discussed his scheme with her because he was afraid she would ridicule his plan. Still, maybe she would be glad to have him out from under her feet for awhile. Galvanized into action with more enthusiasm than information and even less skill, John Shaback got a few supplies together and hired a truck to take him and his gear to Cooking Lake, just outside Edmonton.

On a bright brisk morning, the pilot helped him load his small supply of grub, traps and winter supplies. Because John had assured the pilot he was flying to "A" lake, the pilot assumed that his passenger was familiar with the lay of the land. He didn't file a flight plan because John was positive it was not very far from Edmonton. This was the first of many tragic mistakes for John. They took off on September 10th.

As time passed, Shaback became aware of the changes of the contour of the land. For the past two hours all that could be seen was bush and then heavy timber. He stared out the window overlooking the miles of wilderness. Suddenly, he saw the reflection of a sizable lake. Quickly he motioned to the pilot to circle and put the plane down, for he saw what seemed to be a likely spot to set up camp, with a small pond nearby. So down they glided, landing softly on the lake, and taxied to the shore.

The pilot cut the engine and glanced at John. He asked him if he thought this was the place his friend had gone trapping from. John didn't know as there was no evidence of a cabin but it looked good to him and with the naive confidence of a greenhorn, he started to gather together his gear. He assured the pilot that it wouldn't be hard to find the trapper as it looked like a rich area.

When Shaback's supplies were unloaded and piled on the bank, the pilot climbed back into his plane, warmed up the motor and taxied out to the far end of the lake. Then with a roar, he took off over the spot where John stood alone. He circled, dipped his wing in a gesture of goodbye and flew out of sight returning south to Alberta.

John experienced a feeling of finality but also he felt free and alive. Leaving his belongings where they were unloaded, he climbed up a nearby hill to survey his surroundings. All he could see was dense forest, spruce and pine with the occasional willow where it was swampy. He thought, this is the perfect place. He had shelter in the forest and a lake nearby for water and food and no one to tell him what to do or how to do it. Finally, he was master of his fate. Such was his outlook on life on September 10th. Glad to be alone and too tired to make a fire or a meal, he spread out his ground sheet and lay down. Finishing off his sandwiches, he curled up and went to sleep under the stars.

Next morning, he ate breakfast and started a search to see if he could find anyone near, but after walking all day he returned to his pile of belongings, sat down and decided right then and there that he had to build a shelter. It was September 12th.

The following day he went hunting, shot two chickens (willow grouse) and a duck but after walking all day, he was pretty tired, so he went to sleep in his sleeping bag. When he awoke in the morning, the ground was covered with ten inches of snow, nearly up to his knees.

The next three days were bad. The wind kept moving the clouds and rain followed. It was hard for him to accomplish very much at all.

John put in the next week cutting logs for his proposed cabin and, on September 26th, he had the frame built. It was 12 feet x 10 feet x 7 feet. Two days later, he finished the roof, put a cloth over a hole for a window and a tent over the door opening. He decided to make a fire but the smoke nearly ate his eyes out. He tried to make a fireplace using the ground (from his floor) but with no stones and the earth so hard, it was impossible. The earth just crumbled in his hands.

John was lucky to have snowshoes, but although he walked miles, he saw nothing. He checked and found he had two and a half dozen cartridges. Smiling to himself, he thought he likely looked like a village uncle in the Old Country, with his big beard and moustache.

Nothing unusual happened for the next two weeks. John would catch the odd fish which he hung outside to freeze but a martin came and stole his trophy. Upon reflecting on his lack of preparation, he admitted to himself that he really wasn't prepared to stay very long but how could he return home? He started to keep a diary.

October brought more snow. John finished the chimney of his fireplace but when the fire burned, some of the earth fell in on him, causing him a terrible headache.

Forty-seven days passed without John seeing a living soul. With the days getting shorter and colder, he had no light to speak of. He started to worry about how he could get out of the North but he was quite sure that God would give him some means to return home.

John had been keeping this diary but now he was running out of paper and there was little light except from the fireplace as all his candles were done. As well, he had frozen toes but then he discovered a way of keeping them from freezing again by putting two pairs of socks in his moccasins. Next he put on his big boots and then he covered them with rabbit skins. He said to himself, now I can whistle at the cold, which was –50° F.

"Exactly two months since my arrival," he wrote. 'Tomorrow is the new moon." With nothing to write about except frost and winter John sat beside his fireplace and read the Bible: "Blessed is he who listens to the words of the prophets." (Isaac 1:8) John resented the fact that many people who don't believe in God make thousands of dollars and he had no luck to make one hundred. The animals were springing the traps but not getting caught.

On December 2nd, John had the worst luck. A wolverine had come across his trap line and taken the rabbit that had been caught. Not only that, but he had sprung all the other traps. Poor John's morale hit rock bottom. He stayed in his cabin all day while it snowed another foot. He had no light but decided he'd try to make something, so he took the fat from the ducks and burned it. Not the best light but better than sitting in the dark all day.

John took stock of his food supplies: he had 50 lbs. of flour, 10 lbs. of sugar, 5 lbs. of butter, 11 lbs. of milk powder, 1 lb. tea and coffee, 7 tins sardines, 1 lb. of beans and one rabbit. Once again he quoted from the scriptures: "God's eyes are on those who fear him and who carry out his wishes."

All this time John's wife was wondering where he could be. Routine inquiry was made to Ottawa concerning a certain individual whose wife was becoming anxious as to his whereabouts. Not hearing from him, she requested the assistance of the RCMP to try and locate him. Somehow John's wife found out he was supposed to meet a man in the Yukon and they were to trap together in the winter. The wife also discovered that the trapper's name was Nazaar. This information proved negative but in the meantime, information was received that there was a trapper named Nazaar who was using poison to catch martin. This complaint was sent to J. Reid, RCMP Liard Detachment and he was advised that the Police plane would be coming to Liard and that permission had been granted to use the plane to check on this latest complaint.

So Reid and his Special Constable, Willie, loaded their equipment and four dogs onto the plane and took off with John Nesbitt, the pilot, to search for the suspected trapper. After a two hour flight, they saw a small cabin on the shores of a lake.

On landing, they found the cabin to be empty but a trail was seen leading across the lake. Searching the cabin, the police found 100 marten hanging from the ceiling, also 20 beaver, the latter having been taken out of season in that area. The illegal beaver pelts were placed in the plane and marked. In the morning, the Special Constable and Reid harnessed up the dogs to haul their equipment while the two men followed on snowshoes.

About 11 a.m. the police plane flew overhead and the pilot, John Nesbitt, called down that Nazaar had arrived back at camp. Returning to the camp, the police asked if Nazaar had seen any other trappers in the area but he had not. During the evening, Jim Reid discussed trapping but no mention was made of the beaver pelts. A check of the marten revealed no sign of poison being used, and they were cleared OK. Jim gave Nazaar time to mention he had acquired beaver hides but when no mention was made, he told Nazaar he had confiscated his beaver and had them on the plane. Nazaar tried to tell them he had trapped them for meat but that was untrue as he already had a winter's supply of food on hand and in his cache.

Nazaar was informed he would be picked up by RCMP plane in the spring and taken to Watson Lake where he'd be tried for illegal trapping of beaver. This was done, he was found guilty, the beaver confiscated and his trapping license canceled—for the Yukon.

In the meantime, John Shaback was having an especially tough time. He had broken the handle of his best axe and his smaller axe wouldn't get sharp regardless of how often he tried. He had used it to cut earth. It was now December 9th.

On December 11th, John did a foolhardy thing. He took a short cut across the mountain to save two miles. That was at 2 p.m., and the sun goes down at 3 p.m. Not seeing well, John nearly slipped down the mountain; that gave him a terrible fright. He would have fallen nearly 90 feet but he hung onto a tough little cedar growing out of the rocks and managed to crawl on his hands and knees to safety.

When he returned to the warmth and safety of his cabin, John faced the truth: he had to go home. He talked to God and wondered why things had gone bad for him and yet people who do not believe in God, they fared so well. He quoted to himself, 'Who give God the most, will receive the most from God.' "Tomorrow, I will cut the wood for a sleigh and then I will start home. If it is God's will that I should not be richer, it is difficult but that is how it has to be, it is impossible to go against God's will."

December 15th: John looked around his cabin. Only 10 days to Xmas and I wonder how this Xmas will be for me. There is still some bread—I opened the 50 lb. sack, 5 lbs. of sugar and 7 tins milk and 1 lb. tea, no meat. I still have 3 lbs. butter—so I bake the bread and use the same butter for a light.

December 16th: I quit smoking. I still had tobacco for another two months but I threw it all in the snow and burned it up. It was hard to do but it is bad for health—and I cough a lot.

John Shabak's homemade sled

December 17th: Caught a large marten today. I worked all day making the sleigh, just have to sew around the sleeping bag with the rabbit skins so I'll be able to sleep in the bush. It looks like I'll be on the road New Year's Day. I wish I had brought more food.

December 20th: Today I suffer from hunger—no meat. I shot two chickens but couldn't find them. Every minute I am thinking about the long road over which I will travel and I am worrying.

December 23rd: I am taking 3 dozen traps, 11 marten, 3 mink, 4 weasels. My earnings may reach $1,500.00. I plan to leave on Xmas day. I will sing carols, then pull the sleigh.

December 24th: I am ready for everything for tomorrow morning to leave this place—my cabin on which I worked so hard and so long. When I sing the carols, I will thank God for all his blessings up to now. It was a proper Lent, only fish to eat.

122

December 25th: Today, Christmas Day, left the cabin, started on the road, not a whole can of milk, 2 lbs. sugar, nearly full can of butter and 20 lbs. flour. This is all I have. Frost is –35° F.; cold biting wind; sweating; hard to walk; so much snow; maybe 4-5 miles a day. No food except 1 lb. milk, 7 lbs. flour, that's all I have. Frost is –35°; very biting. I do not know what will be if I do not meet anybody. Already got through the terrible snow; at first I have to make a trail, then come back and take the sleigh and pull it. The situation is serious but there is one hope that God will keep me by some means and will save me. It is a fright, a death by starvation and I cannot keep my mind at peace.

John Shaback had left Edmonton in September in search of a new life and it wasn't until the following spring that his wife became sufficiently alarmed that she reported him as a missing person. Even then, it was because of her nagging relatives. She had heard reports that he had taken off with another woman and was not as alarmed as she was hurt by his absence. Finally, she filed a missing person report that circulated throughout the provinces and copies were filed with the RCMP.

Because our spring mail schedule was in early March, before the ice went out, we did not receive the notice until the July mail. The end of the first week of July, after receiving the bulletin, Jim and Willie, his half native interpreter, made a patrol to South Nahanni where they visited the trading post of the Turner brothers, Stan and Dick.

Jim mentioned the disappearance of a man from Edmonton, and the Turners told him that in late winter, some of the younger natives had gone up the Nahanni River to set traps. On the front of one of their old out-cabins they had found a soldier's cap on a nail and a note that read, "Dead Man Here."

They took off and never looked back until they reached their parent's home camp, where they reported their discovery. The senior members decided to make a trip back up the river where the young men had gotten their terrible fright.

They discovered sheets of paper strewn around the cabin and in the immediate area outside. Signs around suggested to them that

Shaback's cap on a homemade cross sign reads "Deadman Here"

bears had discovered the remains of a human body and had dragged it outside where they finished it off, leaving the larger bones scattered nearby.

Cautiously, the natives gathered everything up and put the remains in a pail, hanging it from a rafter in the cabin. They then returned to their base camp and trap line, where they remained until the end of the trapping season. Later in spring, they went-down river to the mouth of the Nahanni where they related their story to the Turners, who in turn relayed it to Jim and Willie. The two men decided that a trip up the river was necessary but first they would have to return home to make preparations as the trip would take about a week.

Recovery

Clarence, a newly appointed Game Warden from Alberta, and a greenhorn to the North, was very keen to go on the trip. He knew where the bad spots were on the river and as any information was very welcome, Clarence was included in the plans. Two days later the three men, Jim, Willie and Clarence set off in an eighteen foot freighter canoe with two nine horsepower kickers attached to the stern. It was eighty miles to the junction where the Nahanni River flowed into the Liard . Reaching it, they turned and headed up towards the Hot Springs. They stopped there at the cabin of an old trapper friend named Gus Kraus. Gus warned them of very fast water ahead but Clarence assured the men that he knew all the dangerous spots. He wasn't at all concerned that he couldn't swim.

124

Off they started against the fast flowing river which was flanked on both sides by sheer cliffs of rock walls rising about 1,500 feet from the edge of the water. Numerous canyons ran in different directions. Coming around a sharp bend in the river, they found themselves confronted by a wall of white-water rapids. Clarence had forgotten about that area. Too late, they were thrown against the stone wall where the boiling water hit the bank at a right angle, then curled back to the river. Suddenly, a huge wave rolled over the big canoe and the motors shorted out. The boat shot backwards down the rapids. The three men grabbed their paddles and frantically worked their way to calmer water.

There they did some quiet thinking, thanking the good Lord for saving them from the wrath of the dangerous river. The question was, what next? They decided to attempt the trip later when the water would be higher and it would then be possible to skirt the rapids. Grateful to be returning home safely, they discussed their intentions for the following season.

Their decision was that next trip, they would hire Joe Donta, a native who was skilled at reading water. Joe was approached to guide them and he gladly accepted.

Nahanni Mountians

Hell's Gate, Nahanni River

This time their trip up the river was successful and on arriving at the dilapidated cabin, they found the pail, still hanging from the rafters. Taking it, they left and returned to Liard, where John Shaback's remains were turned over to the Roman Catholic Mission which conducted a proper burial.

It seems John had stumbled across this old out-cabin on the bank of the Caribou River. It was in February when the mercury had dropped to −74° F. recorded at Snag. If he had travelled around one more sweeping curve in the river, he would have come across a trapper's cabin in which a large cache of food was stored.

And so it was, that this valley seemed to be rightly named, 'Headless' or 'Deadman's Valley'. "Headless" because two prospectors were said to have been discovered headless, still in their sleeping bags. They were the MacLeod brothers, uncles of our interpreter Willie.

The information and direct quotes made by John Shaback have all been taken from his diary found by Jim Reid and translated from Russian to English by the RCMP headquaters in Ottawa. A copy was then sent back to Jim Reid.

January 1947–Shaback's last entry in his diary:

"These are the last words I am writing as I have no more strength. This is my 28th day of travel—sufferings are hellish, it is already the 5th, day I had not a thing to eat, my strength has already left me and I am unable to make a fire. Maybe I will live until tomorrow before my soul will fly away—already cramps in the stomach have started, ends of my fingers are frozen off. The clothing on me is nearly burned off. Unbelievable sufferings have come. I was able to sit up today and walked 2 hrs. and I was close to the Liard River where there is a trading post but strength has left me and I have to die this way. I am so anxious to live. This is the most frightful time of my life, and he will, the one who reads this, do not say a bad word about me and it will be easier for me to rest.

Signed J. Shaback

Son of Talymum"

John Shaback's grave marker Catholic church
graveyard, Fort Liard, N.W.T.

Going Home

The time to return to civilization was drawing near and it brought many mixed feelings. They would soon disappear.

We gathered together some cherished souvenirs such as moose hide moccasins trimmed with silk work, and a gun case made of moose-hide, richly decorated with beautiful beadwork on the black velvet background. I personally inherited a lovely moose hide jacket given to me by Francis Arrowhead, Chief of one of the bands. Jim received a gorgeous belt made entirely of porcupine quills, and other articles, now forgotten. We brought out a huge grizzly hide, a silver-tip bear, the distance between the ears being 15 inches, just to give you an idea of his size. Also, there was a set of horns from a mountain sheep. Jim put the curly horns on an ant hill to make sure the horns were well cleaned out by the ants before we left.

We had furs of various kinds: martin and mink for gifts, red, cross and silver fox pelts. I had selected six lynx skins from Jack Sime and had a lynx coat made up in Truro, Nova Scotia. Also memories more precious than material things. But best of all, we had a healthy family.

I knew I would sorely miss the glorious sunsets between the mountains, the softly falling early snowflakes which seemed to add to the beauty of the land and the peace that accompanied it, the sudden chinook winds that brought such welcome relief in February, and the overnight arrival of spring with no in-between miserable weather.

I'd miss the cheery smiles of the natives who didn't say much but nodded their heads and smiled—even stopping to pat the children on the head as they passed.

It was nearly time to leave. It's almost unbelievable that we traveled forty-two days to come here but it will only take six hours to return to the 'Outside'.

Looking back, I saw the changes that had taken place. The lot in front of the house had been an overgrown waste and now it displayed a fenced garden almost ready to be harvested. The bungalow we called home was now painted, window boxes installed, a board walk had been built from the house to the warehouse and off to one side stood the stately wind-charger. We were leaving our home where the children had been taught to live and let live and where we learned so much about another way of life.

We had survived by our own efforts and thus, experienced a new found confidence yet also a humbling feeling—especially when standing under that vast expanse of heaven—how very insignificant we really were.

But it was time to leave. The Norseman plane had been replaced by the Beaver and was waiting at the dock. Goodbye good friends, we will remember you, and how you enriched our lives. We surely missed our little house on the Liard River. And so we left knowing that a good bit of our hearts would remain in that little house where we had spent the happiest six years of our lives, up there in the Great North.

The Last Patrol

by M. Elizabeth Reid

The Sarge was old and tired now
And his eyes were growing dim
He knew this was his last patrol
His old horse nuzzled him.

The Mountie stroked the sweat stained neck
Of his old steadfast friend
"You seemed to sense when we left home
That this might be the end.

Do you suppose we'll meet again
Away beyond the blue
Up where the clouds are always high
Where the sun can shine right through?

Where the trail is so clearly marked
That one cannot go astray
Just follow the signs of Truth and Love
And Faith will show the way."

The old horse lowered his shaggy head
He knew he was asked a question
But unable to answer his master's voice
He appeared in deep dejection.

"How can I tell him," he asked himself
"We're broken, both, in spirit
Our lives are o'er, we've done our job
Have we not earned our merit?"

Jim Reid

Index